THE
LAST
WORD

THE
LAST
WORD

THOMAS NAGEL

OXFORD
UNIVERSITY PRESS

OXFORD
UNIVERSITY PRESS

Oxford   New York

Athens   Auckland   Bangkok   Bogotá   Buenos Aires   Cape Town
Chennai   Dar es Salaam   Delhi   Florence   Hong Kong   Istanbul   Karachi
Kuala Lumpur   Madrid   Melbourne   Mexico City   Mumbai   Nairobi
Paris   São Paulo   Sinagapore   Taipei   Tokyo   Toronto   Warsaw

and associated companies in
Berlin   Ibadan

Copyright © 1997 by Thomas Nagel

First published in 1997 by Oxford University Press, Inc.
198 Madison Avenue, New York, New York 10016

First published as an Oxford University Press paperback, 2001

Oxford is a registered trademark of Oxford University Press

Library of Congress Cataloging-in-Publication Data
Nagel, Thomas.
The last word / Thomas Nagel.
p. cm.
Includes bibliographical references and index.
ISBN 0-19-510834-5; 0-19-514983-1 (Pbk.)
1. Reason.   2. Realism.   3. Subjectivity—Controversial
literature.   4. Skepticism—Controversial literature.
5. Relativity—Controversial literature.   I. Title.
B945.N333L37   1997
149'.2–dc20   96–5509

1 3 5 7 9 8 6 4 2

Printed in the United States of America
on acid-free paper

To Ronald Dworkin and Saul Kripke

PREFACE

The main intellectual influences on this book come from the two friends to whom I have dedicated it.

In the late 1970s I attended a seminar Saul Kripke gave at Princeton, in which he attacked various forms of relativism, skepticism, subjectivism, or revisionism about logic. He argued that classical logic could not be qualified in any of those ways, that it was simply correct, and that the only response to alternatives such as quantum logic, for example, was to argue against them from within classical logic. In any case, he pointed out, the skeptics all rely on it in their own thinking.

Since 1987 Ronald Dworkin and I have regularly taught together, and I have been exposed to his constant insistence that the only way to answer skepticism, relativism, and subjectivism about morality is to meet it with first-order moral arguments. He holds that the skeptical positions must themselves be understood as moral claims—that they are unintelligible as anything else. I would not go so far as that, but I have been led to the view that the answer to them must come from within morality and cannot be found on the metaethical level.

These two realist viewpoints, from two different regions of philosophy, have a great deal in common and have led me to the general conclusion that the last word in philosophical disputes about the objectivity of any form of thought must lie in some unqualified thoughts about how things are—thoughts that remain, however hard we may try to get outside of them or to regard them merely as contingent psychological dispositions.

I have presented portions of the material to various audiences. As is true of most of my recent work, it was discussed to my profit in several sessions of the Colloquium in Law, Philosophy, and Political Theory at New York University. In 1995 it provided material for the Carl Gustav Hempel Lectures at Princeton, the Alfred North Whitehead Lectures at Harvard, the Immanuel Kant Lectures at Stanford, and a Lionel Trilling Seminar at Columbia. I am grateful for critical attention from Paul Boghossian, Ronald Dworkin, Colin McGinn, and Derek Parfit. My research during the time of writing was supported by the Filomen D'Agostino and Max E. Greenberg Faculty Research Fund of New York University Law School.

New York   T. N.
April 1996

CONTENTS

THE
LAST
WORD

1

INTRODUCTION

I

This discussion will be concerned with an issue that runs through practically every area of inquiry and that has even invaded the general culture—the issue of where understanding and justification come to an end. Do they come to an end with objective principles whose validity is independent of our point of view, or do they come to an end within our point of view—individual or shared—so that ultimately, even the apparently most objective and universal principles derive their validity or authority from the perspective and practice of those who follow them? My aim is to clarify and explore this question and to try, for certain domains of thought, to defend what I shall call a rationalist answer against what I shall call a subjectivist one. The issue, in a nutshell, is whether the first person, singular or plural, is hiding at the bottom of everything we say or think.

Reason, if there is such a thing, can serve as a court of appeal not only against the received opinions and habits of our community but also against the peculiarities of our personal perspective. It is something each individual can find within himself, but at the same time it has universal authority. Reason provides, mysteriously, a way of distancing oneself from common opinion and received practices that is not a mere elevation of individuality—not a determination to express one's idiosyncratic self rather than go along with everyone else. Whoever appeals to reason purports to discover a

3

source of authority within himself that is not merely personal, or societal, but universal—and that should also persuade others who are willing to listen to it.

If this description sounds Cartesian or even Platonic, that is no accident: The topic may be ancient and well-worn, but it is fully alive today, partly because of the prevalence of various forms of what I (but not, usually, its proponents) would call skepticism about reason, either in general or in some of its instances. A vulgar version of this skepticism is epidemic in the weaker regions of our culture, but it receives some serious philosophical support as well. I am prompted to this inquiry partly by the ambient climate of irrationalism but also by not really knowing what more to say after irrationalism has been rejected as incoherent—for there is a real problem about how such a thing as reason is possible. How is it possible that creatures like ourselves, supplied with the contingent capacities of a biological species whose very existence appears to be radically accidental, should have access to universally valid methods of objective thought? It is because this question seems unanswerable that sophisticated forms of subjectivism keep appearing in the philosophical literature, but I think they are no more viable than "crude" subjectivism.[1]

To begin with the crude kind: The relativistic qualifier—"for me" or "for us"—has become almost a reflex, and with some vaguely philosophical support, it is often generalized into an interpretation of most deep disagreements of belief or method as due to different frames of reference, forms of thought or practice, or forms of life, between which there is no objective way of judging but only a contest for power. (The idea that everything is "constructed" belongs to the same family.) Since all justifications come to an end with what the

---

1. In general, I'll use the term "subjectivism" rather than "skepticism," to avoid confusion with the kind of epistemological skepticism that actually relies on the objectivity of reason, rather than challenging it.

people who accept them find acceptable and not in need of further justification, no conclusion, it is thought, can claim validity beyond the community whose acceptance validates it.

The idea of reason, by contrast, refers to nonlocal and nonrelative methods of justification—methods that distinguish universally legitimate from illegitimate inferences and that aim at reaching the truth in a nonrelative sense. Those methods may fail, but that is their aim, and rational justifications, even if they come to an end somewhere, cannot end with the qualifier "for me" if they are to make that claim.

The essential characteristic of reasoning is its generality. If I have reasons to conclude or to believe or to want or to do something, they cannot be reasons just for me—they would have to justify anyone else doing the same in my place. This leaves open what it is for someone else to be "in my place." But any claim that what is a reason for me is not a reason for someone else to draw the same conclusion must be backed up by further reasons, to show that this apparent deviation from generality can be accounted for in terms that are themselves general. The generality of reasons means that they apply not only in identical circumstances but also in relevantly similar circumstances—and that what counts as a relevant similarity or difference can be explained by reasons of the same generality. Ideally, the aim is to arrive at principles that are universal and exceptionless.

To reason is to think systematically in ways anyone looking over my shoulder ought to be able to recognize as correct. It is this generality that relativists and subjectivists deny. Even when they introduce a simulacrum of it in the form of a condition of consensus among a linguistic or scientific or political community, it is the wrong kind of generality—since at its outer bounds it is statistical, not rational.

The worst of it is that subjectivism is not just an inconsequential intellectual flourish or badge of theoretical chic. It is used to deflect argument, or to belittle the pretensions of the arguments of others. Claims that something is without relativistic qualification true or false, right or wrong, good or bad, risk being derided as expressions of a parochial perspective or form of life—not as a preliminary to showing that they are mistaken whereas something else is right, but as a way of showing that nothing is right and that instead we are all expressing our personal or cultural points of view. The actual result has been a growth in the already extreme intellectual laziness of contemporary culture and the collapse of serious argument throughout the lower reaches of the humanities and social sciences, together with a refusal to take seriously, as anything other than first-person avowals, the objective arguments of others. I am not going to address myself directly to the manifestations of this attitude, but it is there as a source of irritation in the background—though I don't seriously hope that work on the question of how reason is possible will make relativism any less fashionable.

Many forms of relativism and subjectivism collapse into either self-contradiction or vacuity—self-contradiction because they end up claiming that nothing is the case, or vacuity because they boil down to the assertion that anything we say or believe is something we say or believe. I think that all general and most restricted forms of subjectivism that do not fail in either of these ways are pretty clearly false.

My own opinion is that there is such a thing, or category of thought, as reason, and that it applies in both theory and practice, in the formation not only of beliefs but of desires, intentions, and decisions as well. This is not to say that reason is a single thing in every case, only that certain decisive aspects of our thought about such very different matters can all be regarded as instances of it, by virtue of their generality and their position in the hierarchy of justification and criticism. I shall refer to this as the rationalist position. My aim will be to see whether it can be given a plausible form. How can one reconcile the unqualified character of the results at which we aim by reasoning with the fact that it is just something *we do?*

Every major philosopher has had something to say about this. My own sympathies are with Descartes and Frege, and I will attempt to resist the limitation of the reach of human reason that is found in different ways in the treatments of Hume, Kant, and, on a common reading, Wittgenstein. More recently, versions of it are found in W. V. Quine, Nelson Goodman, Hilary Putnam, Bernard Williams, and Richard Rorty. These forms of subjectivism shrink from the apparently audacious pretensions of human thought and tend to collapse its content into its grounds, so that it doesn't reach as far beyond us as it appears to do. For the most part, I shall be arguing not against the positions of particular philosophers but against a general tendency to reduce the objective pretensions of reason, a tendency that manifests itself in many philosophical arguments—vulgar and sophisticated—and that is a constant temptation to those trying to make sense of the phenomenon. The position I oppose will be this form of subjectivism as I interpret its allure—a position which can sometimes seem the only possible account of the subject, given that we are who we are, but which I believe cannot be rendered intelligible.

II

We must distinguish between general philosophical challenges to the objectivity of reason and ordinary challenges to particular examples of reasoning that do not call reason into question. In order to have the authority it claims, reason must be a form or category of thought from which there is no appeal beyond itself—whose validity is unconditional because it is necessarily employed in every purported challenge to itself. This does not mean that there is no appeal against the results of any particular exercise of reason, since it is easy to make mistakes in reasoning or to be completely at sea about what conclusions it permits us to draw. But the corrections or doubts must come from further applications of reason itself. We can therefore distinguish between criticisms of reasoning and challenges to reason.

If reasoning is what has been going on, then criticism of its results must reveal mistakes in reasoning, where these, too, are universally mistakes. Whenever we challenge a conclusion by pointing out a mistake in someone's arithmetic, or logic, or their failure to consider a possibility that is not ruled out by the evidence, or the disanalogy between two cases that have been lumped together, we remain within the territory of rational justification and criticism and do not cast doubt on whether our interlocutor is employing a generally valid method for reaching the objective truth. This internal type of criticism and evaluation imports nothing subjective.

There is an external form of criticism, on the other hand, which undermines the conclusion precisely by questioning the objectivity of its grounds. One important way of challenging *from outside* what is presented as a product of reason is to claim that it is not the result of reasoning at all, valid or invalid, but rather something else: the expression of a particular personal or cultural perspective of less than universal validity, perhaps artificially rationalized or objectified in an act of intellectual self-deception. Sometimes one can challenge a particular piece of ostensible reasoning in this way without implying any doubt that reason of that *type* is possible. The ordinary charge of "rationalization," like the exposure of errors in reasoning, does not question the claims of reason itself but rather presupposes them. It contrasts the sources of belief in this case with an alternative type of ground that would actually justify them, or demonstrate their truth.

But this type of diagnosis can also take a more general form and can be used to make a philosophical point. Depending on the case, the criticism may aim either to discredit the putative rationally based claim altogether, or merely to show that it is something different, less universal but conceivably better founded than it would be under its rationalistic interpretation. If the aim is to show that reasoning is the wrong method for arriving at or backing up conclusions of the kind under discussion, then one would not describe the use of the correct, alternative method as a rationalization but would instead argue that calling it reason is a misinterpretation. This last strategy often plays a role in the attack on reason as part of the basis of ethics, when the aim is not to debunk ethics but to reveal its true grounds.[2]

On the other hand (to complete the spectrum of possibilities), such diagnoses can sometimes be offered neither as criticisms nor as alternatives but as reductive interpretations of what reason really is—namely, a contingent though basic feature of a particular culture or form of life. The usual set of moves among realism, skepticism, and reductionism occurs here as everywhere in philosophy: Reductionism (a subjective or relativist reinterpretation of reason) seems to offer a refuge from skepticism if realism (the strongly universalist position) seems too hard to sustain.[3] Being a realist about reason myself, I regard these reductive "rescues" as equivalent to skepticism; that is, they are forms of skepticism about the reality of what I myself take reason to be. Their proponents would describe them differently—as denials that my understanding of the nature of reason is correct.

Whether they are frankly skeptical or accommodatingly reductive, these sorts of diagnoses challenge the strongly rationalistic—Platonic or Cartesian—ideal. They may be di-

---

2. See, for example, Philippa Foot, "Morality as a System of Hypothetical Imperatives" (1972), reprinted in her collection *Virtues and Vices* (Blackwell, 1978), and Bernard Williams, *Ethics and the Limits of Philosophy* (Harvard University Press, 1985).

3. I discuss this triangle in *The View from Nowhere* (Oxford University Press, 1986), pp. 68–9.

rected either at a particular category of claim, such as legal or ethical or scientific reason, or they may be more general. A further distinction, of greater theoretical interest, has to do with the type of diagnosis such criticisms offer of what is really going on under the heading of reason. Reason purports to offer a method of transcending both the merely social and the merely personal. And a critic of the rationalist conception, believing such double transcendence to be impossible, may say either that what is being appealed to is really an aspect of the shared practices of one's social, intellectual, or moral community (perhaps a particularly deep aspect) or that it is a deep but nevertheless individual feature of one's personal responses. In either case the claim to unconditional universal authority would be unfounded.

As I have said, such criticisms can be offered in a rationalistic framework. Then one will merely be pointing out that this particular allegedly rational justification of a conclusion does not in fact work, while assuming that such things are certainly possible. The same applies when the target is gradually broadened. Even someone who is doubtful about the claim to rationality in an entire domain of thought can continue to accord validity to the claim more generally and can even rely on it in the course of his criticism. But I want also to discuss the problem posed by the broadest type of attack: by the position that no faculty of such universal application and validity could be found within us to test and support our judgments.

I shall argue that while it is certainly possible in many cases to discredit appeals to the objectivity of reason by showing that their true sources lie elsewhere—in wishes, prejudices, contingent and local habits, unexamined assumptions, social or linguistic conventions, involuntary human responses, and so on—interpretations of this "perspectival" or "parochial" kind will inevitably run out sooner or later. Whether one challenges the rational credentials of a particular judgment or of a whole realm of discourse, one has to rely at some level on judgments and methods of argument which one believes are not themselves subject to the same challenge: which exemplify, even when they err, something more fundamental, and which can be corrected only by further procedures of the same kind.

Yet it is obscure how that is possible: Both the existence and the nonexistence of reason present problems of intelligibility. To be rational we have to take responsibility for our thoughts while denying that they are just expressions of our point of view. The difficulty is to form a conception of ourselves that makes sense of this claim.

2

WHY WE CAN'T UNDERSTAND THOUGHT FROM THE OUTSIDE

I

Because of the way in which doubts about reason are raised, the issue is connected with the limits we encounter in trying to understand ourselves from the outside.

Typically, in challenging an appeal to reason not as an error of reasoning but as a rationalization, we point out that conviction is due to some source other than argument that there is no reason to accept: something that produces conviction in this case without justifying. In other words, we are in the mode of psychological explanation; once we recognize the cause, we see that alternative responses would be equally eligible, or perhaps superior.

In offering such a diagnosis to someone else, we provide an explanation of his beliefs, attitudes, conduct, or whatever in terms that he may or may not be able to accept. If he accepts the explanation, then he may find it necessary to give up the conviction, or he may retain it but withdraw his former interpretation of it—deciding, for example, that it is a conventional judgment that can legitimately express a particular and nonuniversal point of view. What we have offered him is an external view of himself, or at least of some of his judgments and attitudes.

We can also apply this sort of criticism to particular regions of judgment of our own which we have assumed to be based on reasoning whose validity is unqualified or universal. Sometimes we may conclude that, after all, that is not so. It is not unusual in this way to come to believe that some of our moral or political convictions are more personally or socially subjective in origin than we had thought. Whether or not it leads to revision of those convictions, it is an important form of self-awareness.

However, the pursuit of self-awareness breaks down if we try to extend this kind of external psychological criticism of ourselves to the limit—which must happen if we entertain the possibility that nothing in human thought really qualifies as reason in the strong sense I wish to defend. For we are then supposed to consider the completely general possibility that there are contingent and local explanations of the sources of all our convictions, explanations that do not provide justifications as strong as reason would provide, if there were such a thing. And the question is, what kind of thought is this? It purports to be a view of ourselves from outside, as creatures subject to various psychological influences and prey to certain habits, but what are we supposed to be relying on in ourselves to form that view?

Suppose, to take an extreme example, we are asked to believe that our logical and mathematical and empirical reasoning manifest historically contingent and culturally local habits of thought and have no wider validity than that. This appears on the one hand to be a thought about how things really are, and on the other hand to deny that we are capable of such thoughts. Any claim as radical and universal as that would have to be supported by a powerful argument, but the claim itself seems to leave us without the capacity for such arguments.

Or is the judgment supposed to apply to itself? I believe that would leave us without the possibility of thinking anything at all. Claims to the effect that a type of judgment expresses a local point of view are inherently objective in intent: They suggest a picture of the true sources of those judgments which places them in an unconditional context. The judgment of relativity or conditionality cannot be applied to the judgment of relativity itself. To put it schematically, the claim "Everything is subjective" must be nonsense, for it would itself have to be either subjective or objective. But it can't be objective, since in that case it would be false if true. And it can't be subjective, because then it would not rule out any objective claim, including the claim that it is objectively false. There may be some subjectivists, perhaps styling themselves as pragmatists, who present subjectivism as applying even to itself. But then it does not call for a reply, since it is just a report of what the subjectivist finds it agreeable to say. If he also invites us to join him, we need not offer any reason for declining, since he has offered us no reason to accept.

Objections of this kind are as old as the hills, but they seem to require constant repetition. Hilary Putnam once remarked perceptively on "the appeal which all incoherent ideas seem to have." In spite of his perennial flirtation with subjectivism, Putnam himself has restated very forcefully the case for the incoherence of relativism.[1] It is usually a good strategy to ask whether a general claim about truth or meaning applies to itself. Many theories, like logical positivism, can be eliminated immediately by this test. The familiar point that relativism is self-refuting remains valid in spite of its familiarity: We cannot criticize some of our own claims of reason without employing reason at some other point to formulate and support those criticisms. This may result in shrinkage of the domain of rationally defensible judgments, but not in its disappearance. The process of subjecting our putatively rational convictions to external diagnosis and criticism inevitably leaves some form of the first-order practice of reasoning in place to govern the

1. "Why Reason Can't Be Naturalized," in Hilary Putnam, *Realism and Reason: Philosophical Papers*, vol. 3 (Cambridge University Press, 1983). The remark about incoherent ideas is on p. 194 of the same book. See also Peter van Inwagen, *Metaphysics* (Westview Press, 1993), pp. 65–8.

process. The concept of subjectivity always demands an objective framework, within which the subject is located and his special perspective or set of responses described. We cannot leave the standpoint of justification completely, and it drives us to seek objective grounds.

It is not just that in criticizing each part of our system of beliefs we must rely on the rest, whatever it may be. The thoughts that enter into such criticism must aspire to a universality that is lacking in the thoughts criticized. Some of these standards have to be discovered; others are simply those basic and inescapable forms of reasoning that enter into all possible criticism—even when some examples of them are among the objects of criticism: The serious attempt to identify what is subjective and particular, or relative and communal, in one's outlook leads inevitably to the objective and universal. That is so whether the object of our scrutiny is ethics, or science, or even logic.

Is this in the final analysis just a fact about how we think? Or can we affirm that the authority of reason is something independent, something of which the hierarchy of our thoughts is an appropriate reflection? I am convinced that the first alternative is unintelligible and that the second must be correct.

The claim has two aspects. First, the outermost framework of all thoughts must be a conception of what is objectively the case—what is the case without subjective or relative qualification. Second, the task of bringing our thoughts within such a framework involves a reliance on some types of thought to regulate and constrain others, which identify general reasons and thereby advance objectivity. This introduces a hierarchy in which reason provides regulative methods and principles, and perception and intuition provide reason with the initial material to work on.

We constantly move from appearance to reality in this way. For example, suppose you think you see a friend who died last year crossing the street in a foreign city. Logic tells you that he can't be there if he's dead and that several hypotheses would remove the inconsistency:

(a) that you've mistaken someone else for him;
(b) that you were misinformed about his death;
(c) that you've seen a ghost.

The choice among these hypotheses will depend on other evidence, further judgments of consistency, inconsistency, and probability—together with general beliefs about how nature works, which are themselves in turn the product of similar forms of reasoning. The aim is to locate your awkward experience in a world that makes sense not just from your own point of view.

That suggests a familiar way of filling in the domain of reason, but the abstractly described aim of the enterprise, to arrive at thoughts and beliefs that are objectively correct, leaves open various possibilities. The content of reason may be quite rich, including strong methods of empirical justification of belief and various kinds of practical reason and moral justification; or it may be very austere, limited to principles of logic and not much else. More or less of our thought may be about the objective framework, as opposed to being simply part of our perspective on the world. The actual content of rational justification depends on what emerges from the attempt to be self-critical and what we discover cannot be reconstrued as relative or subjective. We cannot expect these matters to be settled permanently, since it is always possible that someone will come up with a new hypothesis explaining the perspectival character of some hitherto unassailable form of reasoning—or, on the contrary, that someone will come up with a credible way to extend reasoning to a new domain, like aesthetics.

One of the most radically austere ways of making the division is Kant's: On the subjective side is the bulk of our forms of reasoning, applicable only to the world as it appears to us; on the other side is the pure idea of the *Ding an sich,* about whose objective nature our reason can tell us nothing—and that includes ourselves, as we are in ourselves.[2] This is the model for all theories that the world, insofar as we can know anything about it, is *our* world. But even this view, which subjectivizes practically everything, preserves a nonsubjective frame in the idea that there is a way things are in themselves, and a way we are in ourselves, which together, even if we can have no knowledge of them, ultimately determine how things appear to us. I don't propose to discuss Kant's actual view; for example, I leave aside the mystery of why it should be possible to have a priori rational knowledge of the necessary properties of the phenomenal world, even if we suppose they are basically features of our own point of view, due to our nature and the conditions of the possibility of all human experience. Is it like knowing our own intentions? But the theory provides a limiting case of the division between perspectival and nonperspectival thought, with all contentful forms of reasoning falling on the perspectival side, and nothing but a pure idea of the way things are in themselves, of which we know nothing, on the nonperspectival side.

This seems to me to be too minimal an objective frame even to support the alleged phenomenal certainties of transcendental idealism. But I believe that if we separate the idea of reason from the idea that its results must carry absolute certainty, emphasizing instead its aspiration to universality, then it is possible to withhold any relativizing or subjectivizing qualification from much more of reason than Kant thinks. In spite of the abandonment of certainty and other obvious differences, the conception of the authority of human reason that I want to defend is very like that of Descartes.

2. I am talking about Kant's epistemology. Practical reason, he holds, tells us more.

II

I would explain the point of Descartes's *cogito* this way.[3] It reveals a limit to the kind of self-criticism that begins when one looks at oneself from the outside and considers the ways in which one's convictions might have been produced by causes which fail to justify or validate them. What is revealed in this process of progressively destructive criticism is the un-avoidability of reliance on a faculty that generates and under-stands all the skeptical possibilities. Epistemological skepti-cism, like selective relativism, is not possible without implicit reliance on the capacity for rational thought: It proceeds by the rational identification of logical possibilities compatible with the evidence, between which reason does not permit us to choose. Thus the skeptic gradually reaches a conception of himself as located in a world whose relation to him he cannot penetrate. But skepticism that is the product of an argument cannot be total. In the *cogito* the reliance on reason is made explicit, revealing a limit to this type of doubt. The true philo-sophical point consists not in Descartes' conclusion that he exists (a result much more limited than he subsequently relies on), nor even in the discovery of something absolutely certain. Rather, the point is that Descartes reveals that there are some thoughts which we cannot get *outside* of. I think he was right—though I also think he might have upheld the principle more consistently than he did.

To get outside of ourselves at all, in the way that permits some judgments to be reclassified as mere appearances, there must be others that we think *straight*. Eventually this process takes us to a level of reasoning where, while it is possible to think that some of the thoughts might be mistaken, their cor-rection can only be particular, and not a general rejection of

3. Though the *cogito* is a philosophical Rorschach test, in which every-one sees his own obsessions.

this form of thought altogether as an illusion or a set of parochial responses. Insofar as it depends on taking the external view of oneself, the discrediting of universal claims of reason as merely subjective or relative has inescapable built-in limits, since that external view does not itself admit of a still more external view, and so on ad infinitum. There are some types of thoughts that we cannot avoid simply *having*—that it is strictly impossible to consider merely from the outside, because they enter inevitably and directly into any process of considering ourselves from the outside, allowing us to construct the conception of a world in which, as a matter of objective fact, we and our subjective impressions are contained.

And once the existence of a single thought that we cannot get outside of is recognized, it becomes clear that the number and variety of such thoughts may be considerable. It isn't only "I exist" that keeps bouncing back at us in response to every effort to doubt it: Something similar is true of other thoughts which, even if they do not always carry the same certainty, still resist being undermined by considerations of the contingency of our makeup, the possibility of deception, and so forth. Simple logical and mathematical thoughts, for example, form part of the framework within which anything would have to be located that one might come up with to undermine or qualify them—and thoughts of the same type inevitably have to play a role in the undermining arguments themselves. There is no standpoint we can occupy from which it is possible to regard all thoughts of these kinds as mere psychological manifestations, without actually thinking some of them. Though it is less obvious, I believe something similar is true of practical reasoning, including moral reasoning: If one tries to occupy a standpoint entirely outside of it, one will fail.

Thought always leads us back to the employment of unconditional reason if we try to challenge it globally, because one can't criticize something with nothing; and one can't criticize the more fundamental with the less fundamental. Logic cannot be displaced by anthropology. Arithmetic cannot be displaced by sociology, or by biology. Neither can ethics, in my view. I believe that once the category of thoughts that we cannot get outside of is recognized, the range of examples turns out to be quite wide.

Having the cultural influences on our arithmetical or moral convictions pointed out to us may lead us to reexamine them, but the examination must proceed by first-order arithmetical or ethical reasoning: It cannot simply leave those domains behind, substituting cultural anthropology instead. That is, we must ask whether the proposed "external" explanations make it reasonable to withdraw our assent from any of these propositions or to qualify it in some way. The same thing is true whether the external standpoint is supposed to persuade us to withdraw a first-order judgment, or to recognize its subjective character (or the subjective character of the whole domain) without changing its content. These are questions *within* arithmetic or ethics, questions about the arithmetical or ethical relevance of the arguments.

To take some crude but familiar examples, the only response possible to the charge that a morality of individual rights is nothing but a load of bourgeois ideology, or an instrument of male domination, or that the requirement to love your neighbor is really an expression of fear, hatred, and resentment of your neighbor, is to consider again, in light of these suggestions, whether the reasons for respecting individual rights or caring about others can be sustained, or whether they disguise something that is not a reason at all. And this is a new moral question. One cannot just *exit* from the domain of moral reflection: It is simply there. All one can do is to proceed with it in light of whatever new historical or psychological evidence may be offered. It's the same everywhere. Challenges to the objectivity of science can be met only by further scientific reasoning, challenges to the objectivity of history by history, and so forth.

This doesn't mean that the results are unrevisable, only that revision must proceed by a continuation of the process itself. Any subjectivist proposal must survive as an addition to our body of beliefs, in competition with those it is trying to displace: It cannot claim automatic precedence. Since it is always an attempt to view ourselves partly from outside, it will inevitably have to provide us with a reason for abandoning or reinterpreting some of the unreduced thoughts that we continue to find plausible from inside.

It is customary to make a broad distinction between the Cartesian, foundationalist approach to the justification of knowledge and the much looser, more holist approach supposedly characteristic of actual science, which dispenses with self-evident, indubitable premises. But I think that this is a superficial distinction and that the ordinary methods of science are basically Cartesian. Where they depart from Descartes is in the relaxation of the requirement of certainty: Rational principles that play a foundational role at one stage may be superseded or revised as a result of rational criticism at a later stage. But the enterprise has a fundamentally rationalistic structure: It proceeds by the operation of methods that aspire to universal validity on empirical information, and it is an effort to construct a rational picture of the world, with ourselves in it, that makes sense of these data. However holistic the process, particular empirical observations can't overthrow general principles except in light of still other and superior general principles that give the observations the necessary leverage.

The scientific project, like Descartes's, brackets or sets aside naive impressions as mere appearances until they can be reintroduced into an overall conception on a firmer foundation, and this foundation requires an analysis of how such impressions arise from our interaction with the world. So science, as Descartes saw, requires that we step outside ourselves to the extent possible; but it also has to employ reason in doing this, and in determining what to make of the data that result; and those thoughts we do *not* get outside of. At each stage of our inquiry there will be thoughts which, even as we acknowledge that they are themselves in some sense part of what is going on in the world, cannot be the object of an external psychological understanding that does not also employ them. There is nothing more fundamental to the construction of human knowledge than the reasoning that goes into the generation and elimination of scientific hypotheses suggested by the available evidence.

This, in outline, is Descartes's conception of knowledge— it is developed through interaction between the two poles of subjective appearances and nonsubjective reasoning to form a credible picture of an objectively existing world. Experience by itself does not produce scientific theories, and the reasoning that does produce them cannot be regarded by us as merely a more elaborate species of subjective impressions. To think that, we would have to take up the view from still farther outside ourselves, and the construction of any such view would have to rely on some thoughts that claimed objective validity in their turn. Such major conceptual revolutions are possible,[4] but they must be based on reasoning that actually engages us. The main difference between this and the Cartesian picture, as I have said, is that there is less reliance on indubitable judgments—though the closer you can get to certainty in scientific reasoning the better, and in its mathematical aspects that aim is achievable.

Descartes's general point remains correct: We discover objective reason by discovering that we run up against certain limits when we inquire whether our beliefs, values, and so forth are subjective, culturally relative, or otherwise essentially perspectival. Certain forms of thought inevitably occur

---

4. Einstein's special theory of relativity is an example. It revealed the space and time of Newtonian physics as subjective appearances.

straight in the consideration of such hypotheses—revealing themselves to be objective in content. And if we envision the possibility of coming to regard them after all as subjective, it must mean that we imagine making them the focus of other thoughts whose validity is truly universal. The idea of reason grows out of the attempt to distinguish subjective from objective. So far as I can see, that is what inevitably happens if one tries to take subjectivist proposals seriously—tries to determine whether they can be believed rather than just uttered.

This response to subjectivism may appear to be simply question-begging. After all, if someone responded to every challenge to tea-leaf reading as a method of deciding factual or practical questions by appealing to further consultation of the tea leaves, it would be thought absurd. Why is reasoning about challenges to reason different?

The answer is that the appeal to reason is implicitly authorized by the challenge itself, so this is really a way of showing that the challenge is unintelligible. The charge of begging the question implies that there is an alternative—namely, to examine the reasons for and against the claim being challenged while suspending judgment about it. For the case of reasoning itself, however, no such alternative is available, since any considerations against the objective validity of a type of reasoning are inevitably attempts to offer reasons against it, and these must be rationally assessed. The use of reason in the response is not a gratuitous importation by the defender: It is demanded by the character of the objections offered by the challenger. In contrast, a challenge to the authority of tea leaves does not itself lead us back to the tea leaves.

We are again on Cartesian territory here: Descartes is standardly criticized for the circularity of the argument by which he defends the authority of reason through a rational argument for the existence of a nondeceiving God. But leaving aside the weakness of his actual proofs of the existence of God, the procedure of replying to challenges to reasoning with more rational argument seems to me blameless. Any challenge mounted against reasoning would have to involve reasoning of its own, and this can only be evaluated rationally—that is, by methods that aspire to general validity.[5]

This is the inevitable consequence of treating the proposal as something we are asked to *think* about; and what is the alternative? Those who challenge the rationalist position by arguing that what it appeals to at every stage are really contingent and perhaps local intuitions, practices, or conventions may attempt to apply this analysis all the way down the line, wherever a challenge to reason is met by further reasoning. But I do not see how they can terminate the process with a challenge that does not itself invite rational assessment.

Such a structure shows itself constantly in the actual procedures of our thought—in its phenomenology, so to speak. The question is, what does it mean? What should our attitude toward it be? How can we reconcile it with the recognition that we are biological specimens, fallible creatures subject to a great many influences that we may not understand, and formed by causes over many of which we have no control? If we look at how people actually think, we find that the claim to objective content is pervasive. It is found even in aesthetic judgment, which (though it is not a form of reason because it does not follow general principles[6]) cannot as a whole be displaced by sociological, psychological, historical, or economic explanation of its sources. But I shall concentrate on reasoning, logical, empirical, and practical. It cannot, I believe, be regarded as merely a psychological or social phenomenon—because that would mean trying to get outside it in a way we cannot do. The question is, how can one regard it otherwise?

5. See Bernard Williams, *Descartes: The Project of Pure Inquiry* (Penguin, 1978), pp. 206–7. If anything, I think Descartes gives the challenges too much credit; see the further discussion in chapter 3.

6. See Mary Mothersill, *Beauty Restored* (Oxford University Press, 1984).

What kind of self-understanding would make our capacity to think comprehensible?

III

I believe there is no informative general answer to this question, because the authority of the most fundamental kinds of thought reveals itself only from inside each of them and cannot be underwritten by a theory of the thinker. The primacy of self-understanding is precisely what has to be resisted.

There is a kind of inequality in disputes about the unqualified authority of reason: Its attackers, in one version, content themselves with saying the same simple thing over and over, while its defenders have to resist with something different and more complicated for each type of application of reason. The resistance must be piecemeal even if there is also a general argument that not everything can be subjective; for that argument does not tell us where in the cognitive network universal validity or rational authority is to be found. (Indeed, the boundary may shift as a result of reasoning.) We have to discover the answer by seeing which kinds of substantive judgments overpower a perspectival interpretation of themselves. There is no alternative to considering the alternatives and judging their relative merits.

The subjectivist's all-purpose comment, applicable to anything we say or do, including any procedure of justification and criticism, is that it is ultimately the manifestation of contingent dispositions for which there is no further justification. Justification proceeds only within the practices which those dispositions support—practices that reflect the common forms of life of our culture or our species, but nothing more universal than that. This argument, whatever it may be worth, can be made about anything. It is always possible to say, after the final justification has been given, "But that is only something that *satisfies* you, something you say with the conviction that it requires no further justification: and all that you say is merely a manifestation of the contingencies of your personal, social, and biological makeup. The end of the line is not the content of your reasoning but rather the fact that for you, justifications come to an end here; and that is a natural fact."

The reply to this cannot be equally general, since sometimes the claim to a more universal objectivity can be shown to be spurious, through an alternative explanation of the process. The defender of reason must therefore mount his defense in each domain of thought separately, by trying to show, from within a form of reasoning, that its methods are inescapable and that first-order engagement with them resists displacement by an explanation of the practice in other terms that do not employ those methods. The general challenge at the metalevel must be reinterpreted as a set of proposals about the subjectivity of particular forms of ostensible reasoning, so that it can be met by multiple particular responses at the ground level. Those responses must show, for the case of mathematics, or ethics, or natural science, that the methods internal to that form of inquiry have an authority that is essentially inexhaustible, so that their results cannot be bracketed or relativized in the way proposed. It must be shown that we cannot have the subjective without the objective *in this case*.

This means that a sufficiently facile and persistent critic of the claims of universal reason has an easier time than their defender. The former can just say the same thing again and again; but the only way to defend the objectivity of ethics, for example, is by ethical argument at the ground level—by showing that it is impossible to get entirely behind it or outside of it. To turn the tables on the subjectivist one must take his proposal seriously, not as an empty formula that can be applied to anything but as a specific claim about the area of thought whose unrelativized authority is being challenged. Only in that way can the clash between the inner substance of the thoughts and the relativizing external view of them be brought into the open.

Here are two flagrant examples of the interpretation of reason as consensus, both of them from philosophers. I admit they are easy targets, but the view expressed is very common. Sabina Lovibond refers to

> our lack of access to any distinction between those of our beliefs which are actually true, and those which are merely held true by us. No such distinction can survive our conscious recognition that some human authority has to decide the claim of any proposition to be regarded as true—and, accordingly, that the objective validity of an assertion or an argument is always at the same time something of which human beings (those human beings who call it 'objectively valid') are subjectively persuaded.[7]

And she credits Wittgenstein:

> Thus Wittgenstein's conception of language incorporates a non-foundational epistemology which displays the notions of objectivity (sound judgement) and rationality (valid reasoning) as grounded in consensus—theoretical in the first instance, but ultimately practical.[8]

Richard Rorty puts the same point this way:

> We cannot find a skyhook which lifts us out of mere coherence—mere agreement—to something like "correspondence with reality as it is in itself." . . . Pragmatists would like to replace the desire for objectivity—the desire to be in touch with a reality which is more than some community with which we identify ourselves—with the desire for solidarity with that community.[9]

7. *Realism and Imagination in Ethics* (University of Minnesota Press, 1983), p. 37.
8. Ibid., p. 40.
9. "Science as Solidarity," in Rorty's *Objectivity, Relativism, and Truth* (Cambridge University Press, 1991), pp. 38–9.

Such views have a self-evident air if they are not examined too closely, which may account for their greater popularity outside philosophy than in it. But if one takes them seriously, they turn out to be inconsistent with the very consensus on which they propose to "ground" objectivity. What human beings who form scientific or mathematical beliefs agree on is that these things are true, full stop, and would be true whether we agreed on them or not—and furthermore that what makes *that* true is not just that we agree to say it! The only way to deal with such a general subjectivist slogan is to convert it into a specific, substantive claim about arithmetic, or physics, or whatever, and see how it holds up. I believe it will usually turn out to be inconsistent with the content of statements within the discourse under review, and considerably less credible than they are, in a direct contest.

The standard response of a subjectivist to such arguments is that he is not saying anything that conflicts with the content of ordinary mathematical, or scientific, or ethical judgments and arguments. Rather, he is simply explaining how they really work. Here is another passage from Rorty (I am not making this up):

> What people like Kuhn, Derrida and I believe is that it is pointless to ask whether there really are mountains or whether it is merely convenient for us to talk about mountains.
>
> We also think it is pointless to ask, for example, whether neutrinos are real entities or merely useful heuristic fictions. This is the sort of thing we mean by saying that it is pointless to ask whether reality is independent of our ways of talking about it. Given that it pays to talk about mountains, as it certainly does, one of the obvious truths about mountains is that they were here before we talked about them. If you do not believe that, you probably do not know how to play the usual language-games which employ the word "mountain." But the utility of those language-games has nothing to do with the question of whether Reality as It

Is In Itself, apart from the way it is handy for human beings
to describe it, has mountains in it.[10]

But he can't escape so easily. The claim that there is nothing
more to objectivity than solidarity with your speech community, even if it is extended to the things your speech community says would be true whether they said so or not, directly contradicts the categorical statements it purports to be
about—that there are infinitely many prime numbers, that
racial discrimination is unjust, that water is a compound, that
Napoleon was less than six feet tall.

The contradiction comes from adding a qualification that
is incompatible with the unqualified nature of the original.
The strongest objection to these ideas is the most obvious. The
subjectivist may insist that he is not denying any of the following commonplaces, but he cannot really give a sensible account of them:

(1) There are many truths about the world that we will
never know and have no way of finding out.
(2) Some of our beliefs are false and will never be discovered to be so.
(3) If a belief is true, it would be true even if no one believed it.

Simply to say that such statements are part of the "language-
game" with which we seek solidarity does not render them
intelligible. It is as if someone said "There is nothing more to
wrongness than being contrary to the laws of my community,"
and then added, "Of course, the laws of my community
specify that not everything that is wrong is illegal."

These forms of subjectivism are radical positive claims,
and not, as their proponents represent them, merely the rejection of metaphysical excesses. To take such a claim seri-

10. "Does Academic Freedom Have Philosophical Presuppositions?"
Academe, November–December 1994, pp. 56–7.

ously, one has to try to interpret it as a genuine alternative—something we are being asked to believe about our relation to the world—and then it will inevitably engage the mechanisms of rational assessment. Such a proposal cannot be exempted from the requirements of intelligibility and credibility: It is a statement after all, and supposed to be true. How else can we decide whether to accept it but by thinking about it? In most cases we will then conclude that reason and objectivity are not grounded in consensus, but on the contrary, that where consensus is available, it arises from the convergence among different individuals, all reasoning to get at the truth. There is a consensus on the nondenumerability of the real numbers because the demonstration of it is conclusive, and not vice versa.

The subjectivist cannot save his position by conceding the unavoidable appearance of certain objective forms of thought in our actual procedures of reasoning—conceding the appearance as a psychological fact—while at the same time insisting that this doesn't mean that the aim of those procedures is to lead us to what is true independent of our beliefs. He cannot do this, because such a "phenomenological reduction" would again be to try to get outside of these thoughts and regard them merely as appearances—which is precisely what can't be done.

Attempts to relativize objectivity to a conceptual scheme fail for the same reason. Suppose someone concedes that in a sense not everything can be subjective—that in any system of thought something must play the role of that which is objectively or nonrelatively valid—and that we necessarily run up against it when we attempt to class some of our other responses as subjective. And suppose he then suggests that this might be something different in different conceptual schemes or different types of minds, that in any case it seems to belong to the contingent cognitive psychology of reasoning. The reply is that since reasoning produces belief, and belief is always belief in the truth of what is believed, the distinction between the mere phenomenological acknowledgment of reason and the recognition of its objective validity is not intelligible. We can't, for example, just observe from the sidelines that logic provides an unconditional frame for our thoughts. We may of course decide, for good reasons, to abandon as erroneous forms of argument that we once found persuasive. But if reflection and argument actually do persuade us of something, it is not going to be possible for us at the same time to regard that as just a deep fact about the phenomenology of thought. This is merely an instance of the impossibility of thinking "It is true that I believe that p; but that is just a psychological fact about me; about the truth of p itself, I remain uncommitted."

The idea of alternative conceptual schemes is no help here. There are types of thought we cannot do without, even when we try to think of ourselves, from outside, as thinking creatures. We are no more able to get outside of those thoughts when thinking of other possible thinking creatures. So the idea of an alternative mind or conceptual scheme is useless in distancing ourselves from such thoughts: Their content defeats all attempts to relativize it.[11] In the end, I believe, there is no position in intellectual space for the perspectivalist to occupy.

IV

However much one may try to construe one's concepts and thoughts naturalistically, as the expression of contingent

---

11. This is not essentially different from Davidson's attack on the idea of alternative conceptual schemes. Though Davidson's result emerges from the conditions of interpretation, it is not merely a matter of having to see other minds in terms of my own—which sounds much too subjective. Rather, it is the actual content of certain thoughts about the world and forms of reasoning that sets the conditions of interpretation: Nothing could qualify as thought which did not meet those conditions. See Donald Davidson, "On the Very Idea of a Conceptual Scheme," in his *Inquiries into Truth and Interpretation* (Oxford University Press, 1984).

forms of life, the logic of the effort will always generate thoughts too fundamental for this, thoughts which one cannot get outside of in this way and which one must employ in trying to view from the outside anything else that one does. These thoughts cannot in any way be given a first-person interpretation or qualification: They bob to the surface again in their unqualified form whenever we try to subordinate them to psychology, sociology, or natural history. I don't mean that they all have irreversible finality; sometimes they are refuted or displaced by superior reasons. But they form an outer boundary whose interest is nonrelative. My aim is to argue this in more detail with respect to particular forms of reasoning.

There is a further general response that I want to mention at this point, one that haunts all rationalist and realist philosophies. The question may now be asked: Even granting your description of how we think, why doesn't that show only that we cannot *say* that logic, for example, or ethics, is rooted in our natural, unquestioned practices, but that this nevertheless *shows itself* in the way in which arguments and justifications come to an end, in judgments on which we naturally agree? We cannot say that logic depends on such practices, because that would itself violate those practices, in which logic itself has the last word. But doesn't the ultimate authority of those practices show itself in the fact that this last word is the last word in *our* arguments, *our* thoughts, *our* reasonings?

This proposal derives from Wittgenstein's doctrine that the truth of solipsism cannot be stated but nevertheless shows itself in the fact that however impersonally I describe the world, it is still described in my language. I cannot truly say in this language that the world is my world, because in my language that is false: The world existed before I did, and would have existed even if I had never been born, for example. But all this is being said in my language, and that shows that in a deeper way the world is my world, even though it cannot be said.[12]

Why is this not an appropriate comment on my claim that logical, arithmetical, and even ethical thoughts are devoid of any first-person element and admit of no first-person qualification? Why not say that their being expressions of our most deep-seated responses, practices, or habits *shows itself* in the actual process of reasoning, though it cannot be said?

I wish it were enough to reply, as Frank Ramsey is said to have done to Wittgenstein, "What can't be said can't be said, and it can't be whistled either." But I want to reply more strongly that the truth of solipsism is not shown by the fact that the language in which I describe the world is my language, and the truth of some other form of subjectivism is not shown by the fact that justification comes to an end at certain points at which there is natural agreement in judgments. Nothing about the framework of thought is shown by these facts, because the thoughts themselves dominate them.

Everything depends on the outcome of this peculiar contest over the last word. The subjectivist wants to give it to the recognition that justifications come to an end within our language and our practices. I want to give it to the justifications themselves, including some that are involved or implicated in that recognition, which is subordinate to them, just as the recognition that a notation is essential for thinking about arithmetic is subordinate to arithmetic itself. A certain extra step that some people try to take offers only the illusion of a thought, a path leading nowhere: When one adds, "This is simply what I do," or "This is my form of life," or "This is what I happen to care about," to what is in itself not a first-person statement, one adds nothing—not even something that can be "shown" but not said. That this is so can be seen from the fact

---

12. Ludwig Wittgenstein, *Tractatus Logico-Philosophicus* (Routledge, 1922), 5.62, and *Notebooks, 1914–1916* (Blackwell, 1961), p. 85.

that one can add such an empty qualifier to absolutely anything. If there were nonsubjective thoughts, someone would still have to think them. So the formula that simply notes this cannot be used to demonstrate that everything is based on our responses. A tautology with which all parties to a dispute must agree cannot show that one of them is right.

It is hard to be satisfied with giving the last word to certain ordinary statements or forms of reasoning. If one rejects all relativizing qualifications, it is terribly tempting to add something else in their place: "2 + 2 = 4 and cruelty is evil, not just *for us,* but *absolutely.*" But if this attempts to go beyond the denial of the qualification, it may, in the immortal words of Bernard Williams, be one thought too many—with the unfortunate implication that unless something positive can be put in that space, we will be left with subjectivism after all. It would be better if we could just come to a stop with certain kinds of judgments and arguments, which neither admit nor require further qualification. But that seems to demand a level of philosophical will-power that is beyond most of us.

The impulse to qualify is very difficult to suppress. The only way to resist the constant temptation to give the last word—even the unsayable last word—to the first person, singular or plural, is to see how first-order reasoning about the world inevitably dominates these ideas if we take them seriously.

3

LANGUAGE

I

One factor that has contributed to the devaluation of reason is a misconception of the importance of language for philosophy. Since languages are human practices, cultural products that differ from one another and have complex histories, the idea that the deepest level of analysis of our knowledge, thought, and understanding must be through the analysis of language has gradually given rise to a kind of psychologism about what is most fundamental, which in turn often leads to relativism.[1] This is a kind of decadence of analytic philosophy, a falling away from its origins in Frege's insistence on the fundamental importance of logic, conceived as the examination of mind-independent concepts and the development of a purer understanding and clearer expression of them.

Language is in itself an important subject matter for philosophy, and the investigation of language is often the best place to begin when clarifying our most important concepts. The same could be said of confirmation and verification conditions. But the real subject then is not language as a contingent practice but, in a broad sense, logic: the system of concepts that makes thought possible and to which any language

---

1. One interesting form of resistance to this is Jerrold Katz's claim that it misunderstands language, which is not a mere psychological contingency but rather a Platonic abstract object. See *Language and Other Abstract Objects* (Rowman and Littlefield, 1981) and *The Metaphysics of Meaning* (MIT Press, 1990).

usable by thinking beings must conform. The particular contingent language that one happens to speak is essentially a tool of thought: In relation to basic questions, it functions like physical diagrams in geometry, or numerals in arithmetic; it is a perceptible aid to the formulation, recollection, and transmission of thoughts. Understanding it is a form of thought, but it is not the material of which thoughts are made. For many types of thought it is indispensable, just as diagrams are indispensable for geometry; but its relation to the content of our thoughts is often rather rough. Anyone can verify this from his own experience, but it is particularly evident in philosophy, where thought is often nonlinguistic and expression comes much later.

Because language grows in response to the demands of thought and its communication, it will reflect the character of what it is used to represent; but the order of explanation here is from the fundamental nature of things to language, even if in some cases the order of understanding can be the reverse. While there are certainly concepts which are just the artefacts of a particular language, with purely local roots, that is not true of the most important concepts with which philosophy is occupied. In particular, it is not true of the most general forms of reasoning. Those do not depend on any particular language, and any language adequate for rational thought must supply a way of expressing them.

All this is heretical, I know. Yet it seems to me much more plausible than the view that the social phenomenon of language is at the bottom of everything, and the negative thesis can be accepted even without a positive theory of what thoughts are. We cannot account for reason by means of a naturalistic description of the practices of language, because the respects in which language is a vehicle for reasoning do not admit of naturalistic or psychological or sociological analysis. To the extent that linguistic practices display principles of reasoning or show us, for example, something about the nature of arithmetical propositions, it is not because logic is grammar but because grammar obeys logic.[2] No "language" in which modus ponens was not a valid inference or identity was not transitive could be used to express thoughts at all.

Another example of explaining a type of thought in terms of contingent linguistic practice is R. M. Hare's attempt to ground ethics in the analysis of the language of morals: He finds the ultimate basis of the principle of universal prescriptivism in the contingent fact that the word "ought" is used in a certain way.[3] Not only does this take us outside of ethics in search of the ultimate basis of ethics, but it takes us to a much less fundamental level—that of contingent, empirically ascertainable linguistic practices. In this case I think the general response has been that whatever the merits of Hare's substantive moral theory, on the question of foundations he is simply looking in the wrong place. But other forms of the inversion of explanatory values in ethics have gained wider currency— for example the perspectives of sociology, cultural anthropology, or evolutionary biology.

Looking for the ultimate explanation of logical necessity in the practices, however deeply rooted and automatic, of a linguistic community is an important example of the attempt to explain the more fundamental in terms of the less fundamental. It is this pattern of inversion in general that I want to criticize; in its various manifestations, with different social facts in the position of ultimate explanation, it has become something of a cultural norm. I don't mean to deny that language is a system of conventions, or that correctness in the use

2. Not to mention the fact that the consequences of the rules of grammar are determined by logic. Cf. W. V. Quine, "Truth by Convention" (1936), in his *The Ways of Paradox* (Harvard University Press, 1976).

3. R. M. Hare, *Moral Thinking* (Oxford University Press, 1981).

of language requires conformity to the usage of the linguistic community. What I deny is that the validity of the thoughts that language enables us to express, or even to have, depends on those conventions and usages.

There is no doubt that mere custom can give rise to a strong sense of objective correctness, and that this can seem to detach itself from the contingent conventions that are its true sources. Anyone who, with comic exasperation, has lived through changes in the English language that began as mistakes and snowballed until they turned into norms will be keenly aware of this. The use of "disinterested" for "uninterested" or "enormity" for "enormous size" will probably continue to strike me as objectively wrong even if I live to an age when almost no one any longer recognizes them as errors. But in these cases of *usage*, as opposed to validity, one has to recognize that objectivity can't really outstrip community practice.

That is not true, however, of the content of thought, as opposed to the meanings of words. The fact that contingencies of use make "and" the English word for conjunction implies absolutely nothing about the status of the truth that p and q implies p. What is meant by a set of sentences is a matter of convention. What follows from a set of premises is not. This is just another case where relativism is inconsistent with the content of the judgments under analysis.

I also don't wish to deny that consensus sometimes plays a role in determining the extension of a concept—but these are special cases. There is a difference between the instruction "Add two" and the instructions "Pick all the ripe strawberries" or "Don't invite anyone without a sense of humor." There are some concepts like humor whose extension is determined ultimately by agreement in response among some set of persons (not necessarily speakers of a single language)—but it is impossible to think of "Add two" in this way. When we consider the difference between ourselves and the person who, if told to keep adding two, says, "996, 998, 1000, 1004, 1008, 1012

. . . ," the right thing to say is not just that we do it differently, automatically and without reflection, that here our spade is turned, and so forth. The right thing to say is that if this man hasn't simply misunderstood us in the obvious way, so that he can be corrected, then he has a screw loose and is just uttering words rather than expressing thoughts.

It is true that the possibility of a language requires at some level automatic agreement in judgments and linguistic practice: Someone whose usage diverges radically enough from that of his fellow speakers just doesn't have the concept. But such agreement is not all the concept consists in, any more than the perceptual experience by which we identify a physical object exhausts the concept of it. Rather, at some point, for people to learn arithmetic they simply have to grasp the concepts "plus" and "two," and this means understanding that correctness here is not grounded in consensus—by contrast with rules of pronunciation, for example. Whether they have grasped the concepts or not will show up in their linguistic practice, but it does not consist in that practice. Meaning, in other words, is not just use—unless we understand "use" in a normative sense that already implies meaning.

II

One reason for my conviction, oddly enough, is Wittgenstein's argument about rules. Whatever his own view may have been (an issue to which I shall return), I believe his observations show decisively that thinking cannot be identified with putting marks on paper, or making noises, or manipulating objects, or even having images in one's mind—however much contextual detail (including community practice) is added to such an account. Wittgenstein's grocer, with his box marked "apples" and his color chart and series of numerals,[4] is so far an empty

4. *Philosophical Investigations* (Blackwell, 1953), sec. 1.

shell. Such a description cannot possibly explain what it is for words to have meaning. Or to take another canonical example: any reductive account of what thinking "Add two" consists in, behavioristic, anthropological, or otherwise, cannot be right because it could not by itself have the implications of that thought with respect to the difference between what satisfies it and what does not in an infinite number of cases.

Intentionality cannot be naturalistically analyzed, in other words, nor can it be given naturalistically sufficient conditions. It is not to be captured by either physical or phenomenological description. But to say that nothing that happens when I hear the instruction "Add two" determines the correct way to carry it out for any arbitrary integer depends on restricting one's conception of "what happens" to what can be described in abstraction from its intentional content, and then asking for a retrieval of the intentional content from this denuded material—which is of course impossible. The fallacy is that of thinking one can get "outside" of the thought "Add two" and understand it as a naturalistically describable event. But that is impossible. The thought is more fundamental than any facts about mental pictures or how we find it natural to go on. It is a mistake to pose the question by stepping back from the thought "Add two" itself, looking at the words or accompanying mental images apart from their content, and then asking what their content consists in. That is the crucial move in the conjuring trick.

So in my view, Wittgenstein's argument has the force of a reductio, like certain other famous arguments—Zeno's paradoxes, for example, or Hume's argument that no preference can be contrary to reason. However, as with Zeno, it is not immediately clear what it is a reductio of. The problem is to find the fatal assumption that is responsible for the unacceptable conclusion. In Wittgenstein's case, the unacceptable conclusion, as I should put it, is that thought is impossible. The faulty assumption, I suggest, is that to think or speak is simply to do something, in the right circumstances and against the right background, which can be described without specifying its intentional content.

The conclusion that every naturalistic account of meaning simply contradicts the concept is a consequence of the Wittgensteinian paradox that Saul Kripke has expounded.[5] While I rely on Kripke's argument, I am now doubtful as to the right conclusion about Wittgenstein's positive view about meaning. According to Kripke, Wittgenstein believes not only that no natural fact about me makes it true that I mean something— he further believes that this notion should be explained not in terms of truth conditions at all but in terms of conditions of assertability. I am now inclined to think that this, too, is more reductionist than Wittgenstein would have wanted to be. Perhaps the argument establishes only the negative result that no analysis of the intentional in terms of the nonintentional can succeed—indeed, that no analysis of thought should be attempted.

The argument, in brief, is that my meaning a particular mathematical function by an expression—meaning addition by "plus," for instance—cannot consist in any fact about my behavior, my state of mind, or my brain, since any such fact would have to be finite (I am a finite being) and therefore could not have the infinite normative implications of the mathematical function. Whatever we may add on to the mere word, in the way of further states of a physically and mentally finite being like me, will not be enough to determine the difference between the right and the wrong answer to a request for the sum of any pair of integers.

Kripke expounds the problem initially as one about the past: What was it about me that made it the case, on a past occasion, that I meant addition by "plus"? The conclusion:

5. See Saul Kripke, *Wittgenstein on Rules and Private Language* (Harvard University Press, 1982), pp. 73–87.

nothing. So there was no fact as to what I meant by "plus." But there is nothing special about the past; the conclusion is completely general:

> If there was no such thing as my meaning plus rather than quus [an alternative function] in the past, neither can there be any such thing in the present. When we initially presented the paradox, we perforce used language, taking present meanings for granted. Now we see, as we expected, that this provisional concession was indeed fictive. There can be no fact as to what I mean by "plus," or any other word at any time. The ladder must finally be kicked away.[6]

This reveals the argument as a true paradox—that is, one whose conclusion is simply unacceptable. We cannot kick this particular ladder away, and if we did, we would be left without the possibility of formulating the argument for the paradoxical conclusion.

The problem is already contained in the original argument about the past, in the course of which, as Kripke says, "we perforce used language, taking present meanings for granted." But it is in a sense still present in the conclusion, where we say there can be no fact as to what I mean by "plus" or any other word. For the idea of alternative possible meanings between which no fact about me determines the actual one is still behind that thought. And what about the words "fact," "word," "mean," and so forth? We are still "perforce" using language in the attempt to "state" its impossibility. This is not a coherent position: The paradox is extremely radical.

I would put it by saying that the thought that I mean something by my words is a Cartesian thought—a thought that I cannot attempt to doubt without immediately discovering the doubt to be unintelligible. Just as I cannot doubt

6. *Wittgenstein on Rules and Private Language*, p. 21.

whether I exist, I cannot doubt whether any of my words have
meaning, because in order for me to doubt that, the words I
use in doing so must have meaning. In essence, the argument
invites me to conclude that perhaps I'm not thinking—which
is clearly the impossible denial of a Cartesian thought.

It is not impossible to discover that some of the words I am
accustomed to use don't mean anything; but to think this I
must use other words, like "word," which do mean something.
Yet the argument for the Wittgensteinian paradox is perfectly
general: If it works, it leaves nothing standing, including itself. Therefore it can't work. But that of course does not show
us what is wrong with it. That's why there's a paradox.

My response is not a solution to the philosophical problem
of meaning. But I conclude that since I mean addition by
"plus" now, I certainly could have meant it in the past, and if
no fact about me in the past that does not already include the
specification of what I meant can be the fact in virtue of which
it is the case that I meant addition, it follows that there is no
noncircular explanation of what meaning addition by "plus"
consists in. Some complex meanings can be analyzed in terms
of simpler ones, but there is no noncircular explanation, in
naturalistic terms—behavioral, dispositional, psychological, or
physiological—of meaning in general.

The crucial problem is not just the disparity between the
finiteness of physical or psychological states and the infinite
implications of meaning, but, as Kripke points out, the gap
between the nonnormative and the normative.[7] Meaning implies the difference between right and wrong answers or applications. Behavioral, dispositional, or experiential facts have
no such implications. Therefore the former cannot consist in
the latter. It is a straightforward instance of Hume's is-ought
gap.[8]

7. Ibid., pp. 22–3.
8. *A Treatise of Human Nature*, book 3, part 1, sec. 1.

A naturalistic account of the normative is not possible in ethics, either, but that topic will be taken up properly later on. Here, the claim is that the Wittgensteinian paradox reveals it to be a mistake to think of someone's meaning something by a word as a natural fact about him that can be analyzed in non-normative, nonintentional terms. "Meaning it is not a process which accompanies a word. For no *process* could have the consequences of meaning."[9] I do mean addition by "plus"; it is in a perfectly good sense a fact about me. But in response to the question "What fact?" it is a mistake to try to answer except perhaps by further defining "addition" for someone who may be unfamiliar with the term. It is a mistake to try to escape from the normative, intentional idiom to a plane that is "factual" in a different, reductive sense.

The move from the terrain of truth conditions to the terrain of assertability conditions does not seem to me an advance. So long as these, too, are described naturalistically, in terms of how people find it natural to go on and what they agree in doing "blindly," without need of further justification, I do not see how they can be regarded as giving an adequate account of the phenomenon of meaning. It is patently insufficient to say, in answer to the question how a finite being can grasp a concept like addition, which has infinite implications, that it is simply part of the common usage of the term that we are warranted in ascribing that infinite concept to a person who applies it in accordance with common practice in a finite number of appropriate cases. I can't believe that was Wittgenstein's view; it seems to me just as reductionist as a corresponding theory of finite naturalistic truth-conditions for meaning. Crispin Wright underlines the radical character of this position with respect to the possibility of truth outrunning assertibility:

---

9. Wittgenstein, *Philosophical Investigations*, p. 218.

How can a sentence be undetectably true unless the rule embodied in its content—the condition the world has to satisfy to confer truth upon it—can permissibly be thought of as extending, so to speak, of itself into areas where we cannot follow it and there determining, without any contribution from us or our reactive natures, that a certain state of affairs complies with it?[10]

P. F. Strawson expresses the resistance to the "Wittgensteinian" story very effectively: It is an "externalist" point of view on our language and therefore false to the phenomena.

As thinkers and speakers ourselves, confronted with the claim that the Wittgensteinian picture exhausts the phenomena, says all there is to say, we may well find the claim impossible to believe, may well be tempted to say that it simply is not true to our most evident experience; for, we may be tempted to say, we do not merely experience compulsions, merely find it natural to say, in general what (we can observe that) others say too, or to agree with this or to question that; rather, we understand the meaning of what we say and hear well enough to be able, sometimes at least, to recognize, in what is said, inconsistencies and consequences which are attributable solely to the sense or meaning of what is said.[11]

III

I would like to be able to understand Wittgenstein's position in a resolutely antireductionist way that did not leave it open to such objections. The trouble is that some of his most frequently quoted remarks seem to encourage us to go on beyond the point at which he maintains there is nothing more to

10. *Truth and Objectivity* (Harvard University Press, 1992), p. 228.
11. *Skepticism and Naturalism: Some Varieties* (Columbia University Press, 1983), pp. 90-1.

be said; and we would have to explain why that is a misunderstanding. For instance:

> "How am I able to obey a rule?"—if this is not a question about causes, then it is about the justification for my following the rule in the way I do.
>
> If I have exhausted the justifications I have reached bedrock, and my spade is turned. Then I am inclined to say: "This is simply what I do."

> "All the steps are really already taken" means: I no longer have any choice. The rule, once stamped with a particular meaning, traces the lines along which it is to be followed through the whole of space.—But if something of this sort really were the case, how would it help?
>
> No; my description only made sense if it was to be understood symbolically.—I should have said: *This is how it strikes me.*
>
> When I obey a rule, I do not choose.
>
> I obey the rule *blindly*.[12]

It is true that at a certain point justifications come to an end, and that at that point I draw conclusions without further justification. I do not require further justification, because I have been told what to do. But the slogans "This is simply what I do" and "I obey the rule blindly" suggest a faulty picture, which I think can't be in accord with Wittgenstein's intentions.[13] They suggest that the final and correct conception of what I am doing when I add, for example, is that I am simply producing responses which are natural to me, which I cannot help giving in the circumstances (including the circumstances of my having been taught in a certain way). But to think this would be to get outside of my arithmetical thoughts in a way

---

12. *Philosophical Investigations*, secs. 217, 219.

13. For an illuminating presentation of a similar view, see Stanley Cavell, "The Argument of the Ordinary," in his *Conditions Handsome and Unhandsome* (University of Chicago Press, 1990). He emphasizes the easily overlooked fact that Wittgenstein says only that he is *inclined* to say: "This is simply what I do." He stops short of actually saying it.

that would be inconsistent with them. My final judgment must be simply the arithmetical one, not the thought "This is simply what I do."

Perhaps it is possible to understand the statement "I obey the rule blindly" in this way: It might be said that if I think that what I'm doing is just something I can't help, I am not really obeying the rule of *addition* blindly. To obey it blindly could be taken to mean simply drawing the conclusion which it mandates, with no further explanation than that that is the right answer.

This leaves Wittgenstein without a positive theory of meaning or entailment, but perhaps that is just as well, given much of what he says about the aim of philosophy. We can understand him to claim that a certain level of agreement in usage and in judgments is a *necessary* condition for meaning, and for the possibility of giving sense to the distinction between correct and incorrect—but that this cannot be turned into a *sufficient* condition—either a truth condition or an assertability condition. This would be in effect to accept the reassurance Wittgenstein offers at section 242: "If language is to be a means of communication there must be agreement not only in definitions but also (queer as this may sound) in judgments. *This seems to abolish logic, but does not do so*" (my italics).

That makes the view much less startling, though it does require us to reject the question "What *is* it to mean addition by 'plus'?" as one that cannot be given a nontrivial answer. If that is so, then Wittgenstein's name has been taken in vain to endorse relativistic positions.

Barry Stroud has stated effectively the impossible demand to which all failed theories of meaning, including those perhaps misascribed to Wittgenstein, are responses:

> We think we must find some facts, the recognition of which would not require that we already speak and understand a language, and some rules which would tell us what, given those facts, it was correct to say. Familiar, everyday state-

ments of what a particular expression means cannot serve. They make essential use of words that are already "alive", that already have a meaning, so they seem incapable of explaining in the right way how any words come to have any meaning or come to be understood at all.[14]

It is this perpetual desire to get outside of our thoughts that we must find some way of resisting, and it is pretty clear that the best interpretation of Wittgenstein should show him as offering us a way to do that. One interpreter who makes this claim is Cora Diamond, who explains Wittgenstein's opposition to the traditional enterprise of philosophy as follows:

> The demands we make for philosophical explanations come, seem to come, from a position in which we are as it were looking down onto the relation between ourselves and some reality, some kind of fact or real possibility. We think that we mean something by our questions about it. Our questions are formed from notions of ordinary life, but the ways we usually ask and answer questions, our practices, our interests, the forms our reasoning and inquiries take, look from such a position to be the 'rags.' Our own linguistic constructions, cut free from the constraints of their ordinary functioning, take us in: the characteristic form of the illusion is precisely of philosophy as an area of inquiry, in the sense in which we are familiar with it.[15]

14. "Wittgenstein on Meaning, Understanding, and Community," in R. Haller and J. Brandl, eds., *Wittgenstein—Towards a Re-Evaluation: Proceedings of the 14th International Wittgenstein-Symposium* (Hölder-Pichler-Tempsky, 1990), p. 35.

15. *The Realistic Spirit* (MIT Press, 1991), pp. 69–70. The 'rags' are those referred to in *Philosophical Investigations* sec. 52: "If I am inclined to suppose that a mouse has come into being by spontaneous generation out of grey rags and dust, I shall do well to examine those rags very closely to see how a mouse may have hidden in them, how it may have got there and so on. But if I am convinced that a mouse cannot come into being from these things, then this investigation will perhaps be superfluous. But first we must learn to understand what it is that opposes such an examination of details in philosophy."

But if that is Wittgenstein's intention, his method of looking at the details of linguistic practice doesn't seem to me to have the desired effect. I, at least, am left with the feeling that there must be much more to it—some recognition that these practices reach far beyond themselves.

This may seem incoherent. How can I form the idea that our linguistic practices reach "beyond themselves"? It looks as if I am here cutting my words free of the constraints of their ordinary function and assuming that they will still work—that I have a concept of *addition,* for example, which is independent of the ordinary conditions of the application of that word, and which it is mysterious that those conditions should enable us to capture. Is it not absurd to ask, "How can a finite practice such as my everyday use of the word 'addition' enable me to refer to the infinite function *addition?*" The second occurrence, after all, is just one of my uses of the word. I cannot possibly use a concept to cast doubt on its normal conditions of application!

But matters are more complicated than this. When the normal conditions of application seem insufficient to support the content of a powerful concept, it is possible that we have misinterpreted the concept, but it is also possible that we have misunderstood the conditions of application. I think this may be what happens when we take an anthropological view of the ordinary practices of calculation, such as addition. They lose their meaning. But when I *use* the word "addition"—when I am *inside* arithmetic—it is evident that its scope is of a completely different order from anything revealed by the type of detailed observation of linguistic practices that Wittgenstein seems to recommend as a way to cure the transcendent philosophical impulse. What the apparently absurd question does is to reveal the huge gap between this view from inside and the view from outside the language.

I am pretty well convinced by Diamond's claim that when he says "What has to be accepted, the given, is—so one could say—forms of life,"[16] Wittgenstein is not proposing a "given" in the traditional sense of that in terms of which we must try to make philosophical sense of everything else. But how is detailed attention to our forms of life supposed to enable us to escape from the conviction that there is something to be explained here (even if we cannot explain it) about how our forms of life enable us to talk about all those things that are not part of our forms of life?

Ordinary explanations of the meaning of an expression do not explain *how meaning is possible*. Diamond believes Wittgenstein has shown we must abandon the pursuit of *that* explanation as a fantasy—*not* as something merely unattainable:

> Realism in philosophy, the hardest thing, is open-eyedly giving up the quest for such an elucidation, the demand that a philosophical account of what I mean make clear how it is fixed, out of all the possible continuations, out of some real semantic space, *which* I mean. Open-eyedly: that is, not just stopping, but with an understanding of the quest as dependent on fantasy.[17]

Perhaps there is no deeper understanding of the reach of meaning than that involved in our ordinary understanding of the expressions themselves. But then that understanding is not adequately represented by the sort of facial description of our practices that Wittgenstein recommends as an instrument of demystification. I would prefer to say that the infinite reach of mathematical language can be understood only from inside it, by engaging in that form of life. That means that we cannot understand even the form of life by describing its practices from outside. The order of explanation is the reverse of that

---

16. *Philosophical Investigations*, p. 226.

17. *The Realistic Spirit*, p. 69. She is alluding to Wittgenstein's *Remarks on the Foundations of Mathematics* (Blackwell, 1956), p. 325: "Not empiricism and yet realism in philosophy, that is the hardest thing."

in the common (mis)interpretation of Wittgenstein: The rule-following practices of our linguistic community can be understood only through the substantive content of our thoughts—for example, the arithmetical ones. Otherwise they are impotent rituals. We cannot make sense of them by viewing them as items of natural history.

4

LOGIC

I

Most of the reasoning we engage in is not deductive but empirical, moral, and more broadly practical; but I want to begin my discussion of specific types of reason with the sort of logical and mathematical examples that have already figured in the discussion of Wittgenstein's views. Simple arithmetical or logical thoughts are examples of reason if anything is, however difficult it may be to understand exactly what is going on, and they are pervasive elements of the thought of anyone who can think at all. If we can understand how they exclude the possibility of a relativizing external view, it may help with more complicated cases, but all my discussion will be completely general: This chapter is not about the content of logic.

The simplest of such thoughts are immune to doubt. Whatever else we may be able to imagine as different, including the possibility that we ourselves should be incapable of thinking that $2 + 2 = 4$, none of it tends to confer the slightest glimmer of possibility on that proposition's failing to be true, or being true only in some qualified sense.[1] If we are capable of thinking it at all, then it simply cannot be dislodged by any other suppositions, however extravagant.

---

1. Of course I may be unsure of the truth of the same proposition expressed in binary notation; but that is because I am not familiar enough with that notation to be able to think in it directly, without translating: I have to figure out what "$10 + 10 = 100$" expresses.

If, for example, someone says to me, "You only believe that 2 + 2 = 4 because you were in love with your second grade arithmetic teacher," this fails to qualify as a challenge. I may call up the long-buried image of Miss Gardbaum, with her soft hair, prominent bosom, and dark blue skirt powdered with chalk dust, and acknowledge that yes, I was in love with her and wanted to believe everything she told me—but these reflections will be powerless to make me reconsider my conviction that 2 + 2 = 4, because it lies beyond their reach and does not depend on anything which they call into question. I cannot come to consider it, even temporarily, as a mere appearance.

The range of logical and mathematical reasoning is wide, and any particular example may be indubitable to some people but not to others. A good example is contraposition (modus tollens): "If p then q" plus "Not q" implies "Not p." Not everyone recognizes that implication automatically, and some people may have trouble getting used to the idea.[2] Yet it too cannot be called into question or given a subjective reading by psychological observations about how it was learned or about variations in its acceptance or use among different groups. Even someone who is a bit shaky in its application must recognize it as a principle which, if true, has universal validity, and not just some local or perspectival variety. To think of it merely as a practice or habit of thought would be to misunderstand it: It is a principle of logic. Of course it is a habit of thought too (for some), and there are interesting questions about which valid principles it is practically reasonable or even possible to employ in our thinking, given limitations of time and mental capacity.[3] But to think of reason as an

2. In fact, failure to employ it is involved in some of the most common forms of faulty reasoning studied by psychologists. See Stephen Stich, *The Fragmentation of Reason* (MIT Press, 1990), chapter 1, for some references.

3. For discussion, see Stich, *The Fragmentation of Reason,* and Gilbert Harman, *Change in View* (MIT Press, 1986). Stich, however, offers the unhelpful proposal that we should give up truth as the aim of reasoning.

abstraction from the contingent psychological phenomena of human reasoning is to get things backward. The judgment that it is impossible or inconceivable that the premises of a proof be true and the conclusion false relies on our capacities and incapacities to conceive of different possibilities, but it is not a judgment about those capacities, and its object is not something that depends on them.

This is glaringly clear when we follow any actual course of compelling deductive reasoning. It is what makes Plato's example of the boy in the *Meno* so irresistible. When Socrates gets him to see that a square double in area to a given square must be the square on the diagonal, he does so by an argument that is completely persuasive, and we recognize the boy's assent as the product of the argument's validity, which he and we understand: There is no glimmer of explanation in the opposite direction.

Or consider Euclid's simple proof that there are infinitely many prime numbers: If we suppose that there are finitely many we get a contradiction, since the product of all of them, plus one, will be divisible by none of them without remainder but by each of them with a remainder of one. It is therefore either itself prime or divisible by another prime not in the original set. There is no room here for someone to fail to "go on in the same way." If, when presented with this argument, someone said that the product of all the finitely many primes plus one *would* be divisible by one of them without remainder, we could only treat it as either dim-wittedness or gibberish.

We can of course be mistaken in some of our judgments about what is and is not inconceivable. But such mistakes must be corrected at the same level at which they are made. That is, we must come to have some kind of positive understanding that we formerly lacked of how the proposition whose falsity we were unable to imagine might after all fail to be true, and the understanding must be in terms of the proposition itself: Mere external information about how we came to believe the proposition, or about circumstances in which we would have failed to believe it, are not enough.

The same can be said about the judgment that something *is* conceivable. We may think we have conceived of something but then discover that we have misdescribed what we are doing and that we are really conceiving of something different.[4] But again, such corrections must go on at the level of the conceptions themselves. It is not enough to say, "Your inability (or ability) to conceive of the falsity of this proposition is merely a cultural or psychological fact about you." This is a general truth: Skepticism cannot be produced entirely from the "outside." We have to have or develop some internal understanding of the possibility that a belief might be false before any suppositions external to it can bring us to abandon it.[5]

We have here a clear example of one type of thought being superior in authority to others: When we juxtapose simple logical or mathematical thoughts with any other thoughts whatever, they remain subject only to their own standards and cannot be made the object of an external, purely psychological evaluation. In logic we cannot leave the object language behind, even temporarily. We may acknowledge that we are products of biological development and environmental influence, contingently constituted beings with contingent psychologies, speaking and thinking in contingent languages with contingent notations, and formed by contingent cultures. We may acknowledge that in various respects we might have been different, and also that there might have been no creatures like us at all. But none of these thoughts can get underneath

4. This technique is used by Saul Kripke to defend the necessity of certain identity statements despite an initial appearance of contingency. See *Naming and Necessity* (Harvard University Press, 1980), lecture 3.

5. Sometimes external factors may prompt us to search for such an understanding (as apparently happened with Einstein and absolute time). But they cannot provide it by themselves.

the thought that 2 + 2 = 4 or that contraposition is a valid form of implication or that the product of any finite collection of primes, plus 1, is not divisible by any of them without remainder; or perhaps the preferable image is that none of these empirical thoughts enable us to rise *above* the logical thought, thinking about it while withholding commitment from its content. We cannot even momentarily "bracket" the ground-level thought that contraposition is valid and substitute for it the purely psychological observation that we find the falsity of that proposition inconceivable. It forms part of the framework of everything we can think about ourselves.

II

the MATRIX

Descartes himself (in the First Meditation) refuses to recognize this priority. I believe he is wrong to entertain even temporarily the hypothesis that an evil demon may be scrambling his mind to make him think falsely that 2 + 3 = 5 or that a square has four sides. That would require him to think the following: "I can't decide between two possibilities: (a) that I believe that 2 + 3 = 5 because it's true; (b) that I believe it only because an evil demon is manipulating my mind. In the latter case, my belief may be false and 2 + 3 may be 4 or 3 or something else."

This thought is unintelligible, for two reasons. First, it includes the "thought" that perhaps 2 + 3 = 4, which has not been given a sense and cannot acquire one by being conjoined with the extraneous, nonarithmetical thought that an evil demon might be manipulating his mind.[6] Second, the judgment

---

6. A qualification is necessary here. "2 + 3 = 4" is not gibberish. It has enough sense to be necessarily false, and it can enter into reasoning as the premise or conclusion of a reductio ad absurdum. Nevertheless, though one can *suppose* for the purpose of argument that 2 + 3 = 4, or observe that it follows from certain assumptions that 2 + 3 = 4, it is not possible to *think* that (perhaps) 2 + 3 = 4.

that there are two such mutually exclusive alternatives and that he has no basis for deciding between them is itself an exercise of reason, and by engaging in it Descartes has already implicitly displayed his unshakeable attachment to first-order logical thought, undisturbed by the possibility that his mind is being manipulated. In other words, he can't even consider the implications of that possibility without implicitly ruling it out.

Descartes also held that God could have made the eternal truths of arithmetic different—could have made $2 + 3 = 4$, I suppose—but this is unintelligible for the same reason. (See *Objections and Replies* V and VI to the *Meditations*.) He rests the weight of this possibility on his confidence in the idea of God's omnipotence and responsibility for everything, which is greater than his confidence in his judgments of mathematical inconceivability:

> Again, there is no need to ask how God could have brought it about from eternity that it was not true that twice four make eight, and so on; for I admit this is unintelligible to us. Yet on the other hand I do understand, quite correctly, that there cannot be any class of entity that does not depend on God; I also understand that it would have been easy for God to ordain certain things such that we men cannot understand the possibility of their being otherwise than they are. And therefore it would be irrational for us to doubt what we do understand correctly just because there is something which we do not understand and which, so far as we can see, there is no reason why we should understand.[7]

This implies a hierarchy among a priori judgments that is unpersuasive. The idea is that if we believe G, and G provides an explanation of why I would seem to us inconceivable even

7. *Objections and Replies* VI, sec. 8. *The Philosophical Writings of Descartes* (Cambridge University Press, 1984), vol. 2, p. 294 (vol. 7, p. 436, in the Adam and Tannery edition).

if it really wasn't, then it is reasonable to regard I as possible though we cannot conceive how. This makes sense as a general account of how we can come to distrust a modal intuition. The trouble is that in this case, the inconceivability of I is so unshakeable that (by contraposition) it undermines confidence in G: It is impossible to believe that God is responsible for the truths of arithmetic if that implies that it could have been false that twice four is eight. (And it won't help to add that God could also have made contraposition invalid!) Structurally, this argument of Descartes is precisely the same as is offered by those who want to ground logic in psychology or forms of life, and the same thing is wrong with it.[8]

However reasonable it may be to entertain doubts as to the validity of some of what one does under the heading of reasoning, such doubts cannot avoid involving some form of reasoning themselves, and the priorities I have been talking about show up in what we fall back on as we try to distance ourselves from more and more thoughts. Strategically, I think Descartes was right about this aspect of the appropriate response to skepticism, even if he was much too expansive about the range of things about which we could suspend belief.[9] Certain forms of thought can't be intelligibly doubted because they force themselves into every attempt to think about anything. Every hypothesis is a hypothesis about how things are and comes with logic built into it. The same is true of every doubt or counterproposal. To dislodge a belief requires argument, and the argument has to show that some incompatible alternative is at least as plausible.

---

8. Derek Parfit has remarked to me that similar objections could be made to the idea that God is the source of moral truth. The argument against it has to come from within morality.

9. A perennially interesting issue is whether he was right to think we could intelligibly suspend belief in all empirical propositions about the external world. Cf. Donald Davidson, "A Coherence Theory of Truth and Knowledge," in Ernest LePore, ed., *Truth and Interpretation* (Blackwell, 1986).

As a limiting case, suppose someone argues as follows (some-what in the vein of Descartes's evil genius hypothesis):

> If my brains are being scrambled, I can't rely on *any* of my thoughts, including basic logical thoughts whose invalidity is so inconceivable to me that they seem to rule out anything, including scrambled brains, which would imply their in-validity—for the reply would always be, "Maybe that's just your scrambled brains talking." Therefore I can't safely ac-cord objective validity to *any* hierarchy among my thoughts.

But it is not possible to argue this way, because it is an instance of the sort of argument it purports to undermine. The argument proposes a possibility, purports to show that it cannot be ruled out, and draws conclusions from this. To do these things is to rely on judgments of what is and is not conceivable. There just isn't room for skepticism about basic logic, because there is no place to stand where we can formu-late or think it without immediately contradicting ourselves by relying on it. The impossibility of thinking "If my brains are being scrambled, then perhaps contraposition is invalid or 2 + 2 doesn't equal 4" is just a special case of the impossibility of thinking "If my brains are being scrambled, none of my infer-ences are valid, including this one." I can't regard it as a possi-bility that my brains are being scrambled, because I can't re-gard it as a possibility that I'm not thinking. Nor can I appeal to the possibility of a gap, in a case as simple as this, between what I can't think and what can't be true.

III

Impossible logical skepticism is different from the ordinary epistemological kind, because the latter depends on an un-challenged capacity to conceive of alternative possibilities and derive implications from them. The epistemological skeptic argues that we could be in an epistemically identical situation if we were hallucinating totally, or dreaming, or if the world had come into existence five minutes ago. Even under the hypothesis that one is being manipulated by an evil demon or science-fictional brain stabbers, these thoughts about what is possible are usually not themselves supposed to be threatened.

But in skepticism about logic, we can never reach a point at which we have two possibilities with which all the "evidence" is compatible and between which it is therefore impossible to choose. The forms of thought that must be used in any attempt to set up such an alternative force themselves to the top of the heap. I cannot think, for example, that I would be in an epistemically identical situation if 2 + 2 equaled 5 but my brains were being scrambled—because I cannot conceive of 2 + 2 being equal to 5. The epistemological skeptic relies on reason to get us to a neutral point above the level of the thoughts that are the object of skepticism. The logical skeptic can offer no such external platform.

That does not apply, of course, to all propositions of logic or arithmetic. It is possible for a mathematician to have a belief about a controversial proposition like the continuum hypothesis which he neither finds self-evident nor is able to establish by a proof whose elements are themselves self-evident. And on a more mundane level, if I come to believe a moderately complicated arithmetical proposition after five minutes of calculation, it will not be inconceivable to me that I might be mistaken. If I were told that someone had spiked my coffee in advance, or that I had made a slip of the pen along the way, I would suspend judgment. That is because non-arithmetical beliefs about my calculations are essential to the support of the more complicated arithmetical belief. But with contraposition or "2 + 2 = 4," nothing external to logic or arithmetic is involved. Provided I have the concepts necessary to form such a thought, any confrontation between it and any empirical suppositions whatever must be regarded as unreal.

What we have here is a hierarchy in which some thoughts dominate others. The thought that contraposition is a valid form of implication *dominates* all psychological, historical, or biological propositions—categorical, hypothetical, or modal—that might be brought in to qualify, relativize, or cast doubt on its truth. In particular, it dominates the propositions that we learned it in a certain way, or that we cannot help believing it, or that we cannot conceive of its not being true, or that if circumstances had been different we might not have been able to think it. The thought itself, in other words, dominates all thoughts *about* itself, considered as a psychological phenomenon. As with the *cogito,* one cannot get outside of it, and nothing outside of it can call it into question.

Simple logical thoughts dominate all others and are dominated by none, because there is no intellectual position we can occupy from which it is possible to scrutinize those thoughts without presupposing them. That is why they are exempt from skepticism: They cannot be put into question by an imaginative process that essentially relies on them. All alternative possibilities that we can dream up, however extravagant, must conform to the simple truths of arithmetic and logic, so even if we imagine ourselves or others different in some way that makes us fail to recognize the truth of those propositions, part of what we have to imagine is that we would be ignorant, or mistaken, or worse. (And if the proposition is simple enough, we cannot conceive of anyone positively believing it is false, because we cannot attribute both understanding of and disbelief in it to the same person.)

But the consequences of this kind of dominance include more than the impossibility of skepticism. They include the impossibility of any sort of relativistic, anthropological, or "pragmatist" interpretation. To say that we cannot get outside them means that the last word, with respect to such beliefs, belongs to the content of the thought itself rather than to anything that can be said about it. No further comments on its origin or psychological character can in any way qualify it, in particular not the comment that it is just something I cannot help believing, or that it occupies a hierarchically dominant position in my system of beliefs. All that is secondary to the judgment itself.

As I have already indicated, not all propositions we believe to be necessarily true have this status. We can discover that we were mistaken to think that the falsity of a certain proposition was inconceivable—that our inability to conceive of its falsity was due to a failure of logical or conceptual or theoretical imagination. Some of the most important human discoveries—relativistic space-time, transfinite numbers, the incompleteness of arithmetic, limited government—are of this kind. But to reach such a conclusion we must still rely on logic of a simpler kind, whose validity we regard as universal and not subjective. We must find the newly discovered possibility consistent, and if we come to believe it not merely possible but actual, that will be because it is more consistent than the alternatives with other things we have good reason to believe. Not everything can be revised, because something must be used to determine whether a revision is warranted—even if the proposition at issue is a very fundamental one. I am not here appealing merely to the image of Neurath's boat. No doubt, as Quine says, "our statements about the external world face the tribunal of sense experience not individually but only as a corporate body"[10]—but the board of directors can't be fired.

Thought itself has priority over its description, because its description necessarily involves thought. The use of language has priority over its analysis, because the analysis of language necessarily involves its use. And in general, every external view of ourselves, every understanding of the contingency of

10. "Two Dogmas of Empiricism" (1951), in his *From a Logical Point of View* (Harvard University Press, 1953), p. 41.

our makeup and our responses as creatures in the world, has to be rooted in immediate first-order thought about the world. However successfully we may get outside of ourselves in certain respects, thereby subjecting ourselves to doubt, criticism, and revision, all of it must be done by some part of us that we haven't got outside of, which simply *has* the thoughts, draws the inferences, forms the beliefs, makes the statements.

IV

If I try to get outside of my logical or arithmetical thoughts by regarding them as mere manifestations of my nature, then I will be left with biology or psychology or sociology as the final level of first-order thought. This is clearly no advance, for not only does it contain a good deal of material more superficial than arithmetic—it also contains logic and arithmetic as inextricable components. When I try to regard such a thought as a mere phenomenon, I cannot avoid also thinking its *content*—cannot retreat to thinking of it merely as words or pictures going through my head, for example. That content is a logical proposition, which would be true even if I were not in existence or were unable to think it. The thought is therefore about something independent of my mind, of my conceptual capacities, and of my existence, and this too I cannot get outside of, for every supposition that might be brought forward to cast doubt on it simply repeats it to me again.

The subjectivist would no doubt reply that he can avoid offending against common sense, since he is merely analyzing what we ordinarily say, not recommending that we change it. For example, he can agree that contraposition would be valid even if we didn't think it was, because this simply follows from its being valid, and that is something we are all prepared to say, and are therefore prepared to say is *true*. All of the rationalist claims to mind-independence are preserved *within* the system of statements that the subjectivist is prepared to endorse and to interpret as expressions of our basic responses. But this reply is useless.

The reason it will not work is that the subjectivist always has something *further* to say, which does *not* fit into this framework but is supposed to be a comment on the significance and ultimate basis (in human practices) of the whole thing. And that comment simultaneously contradicts the true content of the original statements of reason, and contradicts itself by being intelligible only as an objective claim *not* grounded merely in our inescapable responses.

There is a general moral to be drawn from these observations, a moral that applies also to forms of reasoning very different from the simple, self-evident principles we have been considering so far, and it is this: *Reflection about anything leads us inexorably to certain thoughts in which "I" plays no part— thoughts that are completely free of first-person content.* (This can be understood to include the first person plural for good measure.) Such "impersonal" thoughts are simply misrepresented by any attempt to say that the real ground of their truth or necessity is that we can't help having them, or that this is one of our fundamental and not further grounded responses or practices—to reinterpret or diagnose them in a personal or communal form.[11] And one cannot evade the objection by admitting that such a diagnosis is not stateable within the linguistic practice to which it applies but can be seen to be right nonetheless. On the contrary, we can see that it couldn't be right.

Many thoughts that lack first-person content depend in

11. It is true that Descartes's first step on the road to an objective, impersonal reality is the *cogito,* a first-person thought which he takes to have objective implications. But the philosophical point of the *cogito* is not first-personal: It is that you cannot *stay* with the first person. I think he is right even here, but see Bernard Williams's criticisms of him on this point: *Descartes: The Project of Pure Inquiry* (Penguin, 1978), p. 100.

part on others that have it and that serve as evidence or grounds for the impersonal thoughts. But in explaining how they serve as grounds, one will reach still other thoughts, including those of logic and arithmetic, which are free-standing. While they are had by us, they do not in any way refer to us, even implicitly. It is in this region of impersonal thoughts that do not depend on any personal ones that the operation of reason must be located. Reason, so understood, permits us to develop the conception of the world in which we, our impressions, and our practices are contained, because it does not depend on our personal perspective.

We cannot judge any type of thought to be merely personal except from a standpoint that is impersonal. The aim of situating everything in a non-first-person framework—a conception of how things are—is one to which there is no alternative. But that does not tell us what specific types of thought belong to this finally impersonal domain. What I have said so far is consistent with Kantian idealism, physicalistic realism, or any number of other views. There is no telling in advance whether nearly everything objective rests on a fairly narrow logical base, with everything else coming from particular points of view, or whether great ranges of judgments, including those of ethics and contingent statements about empirical reality, depend on inescapably non-first-person thoughts in their own right.

This is the heart of the issue over the scope of reason, which includes those general forms or methods of impersonal thought, whatever they are, that we reach at the end of every line of questioning and every search for justification, and that we cannot in the end consider merely as a very deeply entrenched aspect of our point of view. I have been discussing particular logical and arithmetical examples, but the real character of reason is not found in belief in a set of "foundational" propositions, nor even in a set of procedures or rules for drawing inferences, but rather in any forms of thought to which there is no alternative.[12]

This does not mean "no alternative for me," or "for us." It means "no alternative," period. That implies *universal* validity. The thing to which there is no alternative may include some specific beliefs, but in general it will not have that character. Rather, it will be a framework of methods and forms of thought that reappear whenever we call any specific propositions into question. This framework will be part of even the most general thoughts about our intellectual and linguistic practices considered as psychological or social phenomena. Instead of logic resting on agreement in judgments and usage by members of a community, the agreement, where it exists, has to be explained in terms of the logic whose validity we all recognize.

Again, let me emphasize that I am not talking about a set of unrevisable beliefs (though I believe the simplest rules of logic are unrevisable). The aim of universal validity is compatible with the willingness always to consider alternatives and counterarguments—*but they must be considered as candidates for objectively valid alternatives and arguments*. It is possible to accept a form of rationalism without committing oneself to a closed set of self-evident foundational truths.

V

What seems permanently puzzling about the phenomenon of reason, and what makes it so difficult to arrive at a satisfactory attitude toward it, is the relation it establishes between the

---

12. Cf. David Wiggins's invocation of the idea that "there is really nothing else to think but that p" (that $7 + 5 = 12$, for example); "Moral Cognitivism, Moral Relativism and Motivating Moral Beliefs," *Proceedings of the Aristotelian Society* 91 (1990–91), pp. 66f.

particular and the universal. If there is such a thing as reason, it is a local activity of finite creatures that somehow enables them to make contact with universal truths, often of infinite range. There is always a powerful temptation to think that this is impossible, and that an interpretation of reason must be found that reduces it to something more local and finite. It therefore may be useful to reflect directly on the employment of reason that gives us our knowledge of infinity itself.

Part of the idea of logical or arithmetical reasoning is that the truths we could ever come to know in this way are only a small sample of the infinity of such truths. The infinite logical space in which known examples are located is given as part of the system of thought that reveals them—a strong case of mind-independence. For example, we know that $(x)(y)(\exists z)(x + y = z)$, but this is a judgment of reason about an infinite domain that at the same time our procedures of reasoning cannot fill out in detail—though it is a further fact of reason that if iterated often enough, those procedures could reach any true proposition of the form "$a + b = c$." The existence of truth in mathematics outruns both decision procedures and proof procedures, but even where there is a decision procedure, we cannot apply it to infinitely many cases: Our capacities are not only finite but quite meager. Even where there is no decision procedure, or we don't have one, we may nevertheless be constrained to think that there is a right answer, and methods of trying to get it which are not guaranteed to succeed.

The infinity of the natural numbers is something we come to grasp through our recognition that in a sense we cannot grasp all of it, while at the same time we see that there is something there which we cannot grasp. So we give the set a name, even though we cannot reach all of its members. Once we are able to count at all, we have the basis for realizing that every number has a successor, larger by one. This is easier if we already use a repeating notation for counting, like the decimal system, which is itself an infinite series; but someone whose numerical language was finite, like an alphabet, could come to see that every number had a successor larger by one, even though he had names for only the first twenty-six of them. (I would guess that infinitely repeating numerical notations were the product, rather than the source, of this insight.)

The idea of infinity would not arise from just any fixed sequence of symbols, such as those used to designate in order the stages of a dance, or the steps that go into building a house. That would not give rise to the idea that every step has a successor. To get that idea, we need to be operating with the concept of numbers as the sizes of sets, which can have anything whatever as their elements. What we understand, then, is that the numbers we use to count things in everyday life are merely the first part of a series that never ends.

This thought is a paradigm of the way reason allows us to reach vastly beyond ourselves. The local, finite practice of counting contains within itself the implication that the series is not completable by us: It has, so to speak, a built-in immunity to attempts at reduction. Though our direct acquaintance with and designation of specific numbers is extremely limited, we cannot make sense of it except by putting them, and ourselves, in the context of something larger, something whose existence is independent of our fragmentary experience of it. Yet we draw this access to infinity out of our distinctly finite ability to count, in virtue of its evident incompleteness. When we think about the finite activity of counting, we come to realize that it can only be understood as part of something infinite. The idea of reducing the apparently infinite to the finite is therefore ruled out: Instead, the apparently finite must be explained in terms of the infinite.

The reason this is a model for the irreducibility of reason in general is that it illustrates the way in which the application of certain concepts from inside overpowers the attempt to grasp that application from outside and to describe it as a finite and local practice. It may look small and "natural" from outside, but once one gets inside it, it opens out to burst the boundaries of that external naturalistic view. It is like stepping into what looks like a small windowless hut and finding oneself suddenly in the middle of a vast landscape stretching endlessly out to the horizon.

And it is precisely by posing the reductive question that we come to see this. We discover infinity when we ask whether these numbers we can name are all there is, whether we can understand counting as just a finite human practice in which speakers of the language come to relatively easy agreement. From inside the practice itself comes a negative answer: The view from inside dominates the view from outside, unless the latter somehow expands to include a version of the former. (There is an analogy here with the philosophy of mind: An external view of the mental cannot be adequate unless it expands to incorporate in some form the internal view.)

VI

It is natural to want to understand ourselves, including our capacity to reason. But our understanding of ourselves must be part of our understanding of the world of which we form a part. And that means this understanding cannot close over itself completely: We have to remain inside it, and we cannot tell a story about ourselves and our rational capacities that is incompatible with the understanding of the world to which any story about ourselves must belong. The description of ourselves, including our rational capacities, must therefore be subordinate to the description of the world that our exercise of those capacities reveals to us. In particular, the description of what happens when we count must include the relation of that activity to the infinite series of natural numbers, since that is part of what our operation with the concept of number makes evident.

So counting, even small samples of it, must be understood as the application of a successor relation that generates an infinite series. Any external view of the practice that leaves this out or makes it mysterious is thereby shown to be inadequate, by the standards evident from within the practice. From inside, the incompleteness of any finite sequence of natural numbers is an evident logical consequence of the concept of number. That internal view has to be in some way made part of any adequate external view.

This is the general form of all failures of reduction. The perspective from inside the region of discourse or thought to be reduced shows us something that is not captured by the reducing discourse. Behavioristic reductions and their descendants do not work in the philosophy of mind because the phenomenological and intentional features that are evident from inside the mind are never adequately accounted for from the purely external perspective that the reducing theories limit themselves to, under the mistaken impression that an external perspective alone is compatible with a scientific worldview. The internal perspective of consciousness dominates any attempt to subordinate it to the external perspective of physiology and behavior, so the "external" account of the mind must somehow incorporate what is evident from inside it.

The strongest refutations of this sort show that even the reducing discourse itself must presuppose the independent perspective of the ostensibly reduced discourse. For example, phenomenalism—the analysis of all statements about the physical world in terms of actual and hypothetical sense experience—is refuted by the observation that the conditional statements about what perceptual experiences we would have if (for example) we looked in the refrigerator, on which it relies for its analysis of statements about the unperceived contents of the refrigerator, are unintelligible unless explained by nonconditional facts about the external world, by virtue of which they are true.

Still more decisive is the example of Gödel's Incompleteness Theorem, the best antireductionist argument of all time. Mathematical truth cannot be reduced to provability in an axiom system, because, first, the fact that a sentence is or is not provable in a given axiom system is itself a mathematical truth (so the reducing discourse itself presupposes a prior idea of mathematical truth), and second, in such a system, it is possible to construct sentences which assert the mathematical proposition that they are not provable in it.

The moral is that any attempt to account for one segment of our world picture in terms of others must leave us with a total world picture that is consistent with our having it. It cannot include a description of ourselves that is inconsistent with what we know—for example that there are infinitely many natural numbers. And the same test applies to everything else, from psychology to physics to ethics. A proposed reduction in any of these domains must be powerful enough to either accommodate or overcome what we think we know from inside them. It cannot prevail simply because the external view of what organisms like ourselves do can always be presumed to be more objective than the internal one. That is not the case; what appears to external empirical observation is not necessarily a more fundamental part of our knowledge than a priori mathematical reasoning or moral judgment or understanding of what a sentence means. Any reduction of these things to something else must leave us with a more credible world picture than one that keeps them in, unreduced.

We seem to be left with a question that has no imaginable answer: How is it possible for finite beings like us to think infinite thoughts—and even if they take priority over any possible outside view of them, what outside view can we take that is at least consistent with their content? The constant temptation toward reductionism—the explanation of reason in terms of something less fundamental—comes from treating our capacity to engage in it as the primary clue to what it is. The greatest monument to this temptation is the Kantian project, which tries to explain the mind-independent features of reason and the world in an ultimately mind-dependent form. I think the only way to avoid such subjectivism is to make sure the explanation is in a certain sense circular: that it accounts for our capacity to think these things in a way that presupposes their independent validity. The problem then will be not how, if we engage in it, reason can be valid, but how, if it is universally valid, we can engage in it.

There are not many candidates for an answer to this question. Probably the most popular nonsubjectivist answer nowadays is an evolutionary naturalism: We can reason in these ways because it is the consequence of a more primitive capacity of belief formation that had survival value during the period when the human brain was evolving. This explanation has always seemed to me laughably inadequate.[13] I shall say more about it in chapter 7.

The other well-known answer is the religious one: The universe is intelligible to us because it and our minds were made for each other. We find this not only in its Cartesian form, as an answer to skepticism, but also going in the opposite direction, as an "epistemological" argument for the existence of God—the hypothesis which provides the best explanation of why we can understand the universe by the exercise of our reason.[14] While I think such arguments are unjustly neglected in contemporary secular philosophy, I have never been able to understand the idea of God well enough to see such a theory as truly explanatory: It seems rather to stand for a still unspecified purposiveness that itself remains unex-

13. For reasons I try to explain in *The View from Nowhere* (Oxford University Press, 1986), pp. 78–81.

14. A good recent statement of this position is John Polkinghorne, *Science and Creation* (New Science Library, 1989).

plained. But perhaps this is due to my inadequate understanding of religious concepts.

3   Apart from Subjectivism, Evolution, and God, what are the alternatives? One possibility is that some things can't be explained because they have to enter into every explanation. The question "How can human beings add?" is not like the question "How can electronic calculators add?" In ascribing that capacity to a person, I interpret what he does in terms of my own capacity. And since I can't get outside of *it*, how can I hope to get outside of and explain the corresponding thing in anyone else? To follow a rule is not to obey a natural law. Perhaps there is something wrong with the hope of arriving at a complete understanding of the world that includes an understanding of ourselves as beings within it possessing the capacity for that very understanding.

I think something of the kind must be true. There are inevitably going to be limits on the closure achievable by turning our procedures of understanding on themselves. If that is so, then the outer boundaries of our understanding will always be reached in unqualified, objective reasoning about the real world rather than in the interpretation and expression of our own perspective—personal or social. To engage in such reasoning is to try to bring one's individual thoughts under the control of a universal standard that prescribes to each person those beliefs, available from his point of view, which can form part of a consistent set of objective beliefs dispersed over all rational persons. It enables us all to live in part of the truth.

5

SCIENCE

I

There is more to reason than logic and mathematics. Subjectivism about logic is directly self-defeating. Subjectivism about other kinds of reasoning can be refuted only by showing that it is in direct competition with claims internal to that reasoning and that in a fair contest, it loses. With respect to science, or history, or ethics, resistance to the external view comes from inside the domains being challenged, though not, as with logic, because they are presupposed by the challenge itself.

The most basic and simple forms of reasoning, in logic and arithmetic, certainly pose deep philosophical problems, but it is impossible to take seriously the idea that they are merely manifestations of contingent and local practices. We cannot think of them as less than universally valid, because not only can we not conceive of their being invalid, but we cannot conceive of a being capable of understanding them who did not also find them self-evidently valid: Nothing would permit us to attribute to anyone a disbelief in modus ponens, or in the proposition that $2 + 2 = 4$.

However, most of the interesting questions which we look to reason to answer are much more difficult. We do not find the answers self-evident, or if we do, we acknowledge that the appearance of certainty may be deceptive. As I have said, this acknowledgment is often appropriate even where we are reasoning about necessary truths. A priori knowledge or belief need not be certain, even though it has greater resources for certainty than a posteriori knowledge. But outside of mathematics and logic, uncertainty is the norm. In most cases, reasoning provides us not with proof but only with reasons for believing a conclusion likely, or for preferring it somewhat to the alternatives.

That is true in science, in other empirical disciplines, and in ethics. The reasons that support a conclusion do not typically rule out the possibility of its falsity, even if they are very strong. And there are sometimes enough reasons in support of consistent alternatives that we may be unsure that the conclusion we have to draw is actually supported by the preponderance of them: We acknowledge that reasonable persons can disagree, and often we can imagine ourselves drawing a conclusion different from the one we have actually drawn. Often reasoning in the strict sense does not support our conclusions directly but only justifies us in trusting or distrusting the more particular judgments and intuitions that occur to us naturally, or as the result of experience. Yet in such cases we believe that what we are thinking about has an answer that is not relative or subjective and that our procedures of reasoning attempt, fallibly, to capture the reasons that bear on that answer in one direction or another.

It is this type of appeal to reason that is most vulnerable to alternative diagnoses and to the charges of self-deception and false universalization. Such charges are sometimes true, and awareness of the possibility should temper our confidence—which must in any case be modest because of the straightforward possibility of mistakes in reasoning and limitations of the available evidence. But they are not inevitably true, and the problem is to give an account of the process that explains this. How is it that in logical, empirical, or practical reasoning that is not incontestable we can nevertheless claim to be using, in a possibly incomplete or inaccurate version, methods whose ideal validity is universal and not relative to anything more contingent and particular about us or our community?

In thinking of this kind, the search for what is universal is itself a regulative principle. That is made explicit in the Kantian conception of moral reasoning, but it is also true elsewhere, for we test our reasons partly by asking whether they are applications of principles that are generally valid, looking for counterexamples, and using both actual and imagined cases in the process. At least this much is true: *Unless* we think that anyone should draw the same conclusion from the same premises, we cannot regard the conclusion as justified by reason. Reasons are by definition general, and we aim always to extend their generality. So part of the question is whether an attachment to this method is itself something we cannot get outside of, as the form of final assessment of our beliefs—including beliefs about what is and what is not a legitimate subject for reasoning, and beliefs about the boundary between the universal and the nonuniversal.

The process gets its start from the bare conception of an objective reality, within which more subjective points of view, including our own, are embedded. At least as a possibility this is inescapable. While filling it out is extremely difficult and in some respects incompletable, it drives us to seek some non-locally valid methods in pursuing it, for that is the only way to subject our personal starting points to any kind of testing to determine just how subjective they are. Further, and more riskily, we proceed by taking ourselves and our experiences as samples of a world that we hope to find, at some level, the same everywhere (in time as well as in space), so that the order we discover in trying to explain what we observe aims toward something broader. There is nothing special about *us*, in other words: Each of us is just a piece of the universe. A vindication of this type of reason would require that we make it credible that the search for order, and some of the methods for identifying that order, will survive every attempt to interpret them as merely subjective—because all such interpretations are defeated by the first-order judgments whose authority they are trying to undermine. That would be structurally analogous to the situation with logic, but without the same kind of necessity in the results.

This extremely general point is so far compatible with the position that the rational base that cannot be explained away is very small—perhaps even limited to logic—and that everything else can be understood as a feature of some more particular type of viewpoint. It is also compatible with the position that reason has a fundamental role in logic, mathematics, and empirical science but that all ostensible examples of practical or ethical reason are better understood as manifestations of specific psychological dispositions. Definite conclusions on these matters depend on more substantive investigation of whether in each domain pursuit of the universal makes sense and, if so, whether it is reasonable to believe that our actual uncertain efforts in that direction are reflections of something that might be further perfected. In this chapter I shall discuss factual and scientific reasoning, but only in the most general terms. The title of the chapter (like that of the one before) may be slightly misleading. I have nothing to say about formal theories of induction and confirmation, or about their relation to the practice of empirical and scientific thinking. My interest is in what kind of thing these theories are theories of.

II

Reliance on reason can coexist with very substantial doubt about the results, and even with radical skepticism. In fact, traditional epistemological skepticism depends on the objectivity of reason: It is always the product of reasoning to the conclusion that various mutually incompatible alternative possibilities are all equally compatible with one's actual epistemic situation, and that it is therefore impossible to decide among them on rational grounds. Radical skepticism therefore has to rely on some thoughts that are not put in doubt and that are assumed to have objective content. But the same must be true of less radical forms of uncertainty—the ordinary limited confidence one has in most of one's beliefs, including qualified belief in scientific theories that are accepted as the best candidates for the moment, even though we know they will be superseded. The reasoning that supports such beliefs must be at some level unconditional also, otherwise it could not show us what might, objectively, be the case.

The general aim of such reasoning is to make sense of the world in which we find ourselves and of how it appears to us and others. We proceed by generating, comparing, and ranking possible versions, and it is these comparisons that are the substance of the process. But we begin from the idea that there is some way the world is, and this, I believe, is an idea to which there is no intelligible alternative and which cannot be subordinated to or derived from anything else. My aim is to argue that even a subjectivist cannot escape from or rise above this idea. Even if he wishes to offer an analysis of it in subjective or community-relative terms, his proposal has to be understood as an account of how the world is and therefore as inconsistent with alternative accounts, with which it can be compared for plausibility.

We do not get to the idea of how the world is from the appearances; rather, we begin with that idea, since the appearances from which we start are ways in which the world appears to *be*. We may decide after reflection and further observation that some of these are *mere* appearances, that the world is not like that after all. But this always represents a modification in our view of the world, based on alternative possibilities and reasons for preferring some of them to others. What we cannot avoid is the idea that something is the case, even if we don't know what it is. Doubts about the reliability or objectivity of our perceptions and judgments have to be based on revisions of our view of the world; they cannot escape it completely. We start from certain impressions about how things are, cast doubt on the objectivity of some of them by further thoughts (including thoughts about our own nature and our interaction with the rest of the world), and reject some of the appearances in favor of other beliefs about how things really are. All of it, including the observations about ourselves, is firmly embedded in a non-first-person framework of thought about the world.

But how does this generate specific methods in which one can feel some confidence? After all, the mere recognition of a distinction between appearance and reality does not supply a method of discovering reality.

The actual procedure is characterized by a high degree of cognitive inertia, and that implies that our actual worldview is to a considerable extent the expression of a perspective. We begin from a natural view of the world and are led to retreat from it by discovering that in one way or another it is inconsistent with our observations. This creates a gap that we try to fill by imagining alternative possible worlds which would, if they existed, be more consistent with what we observe. The judgments of consistency themselves involve logic, but they cannot produce logical proof of the truth of any such picture, unless it can be shown that it is the only picture consistent with the observations—which, given the fragmentary nature of the data, is probably never the case. Our attitude has to be "This could be how things are, given the evidence." The rest depends on whether there are other candidates and, if so, how we compare them.

The driving force behind all empirical reasoning is the search for order. This can take very simple forms, as when I conclude from a dog's markings that he is the same one I saw yesterday. But it leads to higher and higher levels, as we look for wider regularities behind the more specific ones we infer from observation. We don't always find order among the phenomena, but looking for it is the only way to extend our world picture and fill in the gaps between the observational data. The search for order can often lead people astray—sometimes radically so, as with astrology and other superstitions. But the remedy consists in rigorously testing faulty systems by reference to the standard of uniformity in nature, not in giving that standard up.

I believe it is possible to understand the demand for order as a direct consequence of the idea of an objective reality, independent of particular observations and observers. Their observations may be different, but the events observed and the laws governing them must be the same. Even the idea of a single object being seen on two occasions by a single observer implies some form of natural regularity; two observers require further regularity; and the idea of an unobserved but similar event implies still more. And the process does not stop there. A thoroughly realistic conception of natural laws will have to try to interpret them also in ways that are independent of any particular point of view or observational standpoint—otherwise they might be merely ways of systematizing our observations. To be truly mind-independent, the laws—and not just the events they govern—must be perspective-free and must explain why things appear as they do from different vantage points within the world.

In modern physics, this idea constrains the development of theories through a requirement of *symmetry*—that the real natural order should be identified with what is invariant from the points of view of all observers, so that whatever their situation, they can all arrive at the same description of the common reality in which they are situated. The requirement applies not just to particular states of affairs but to general laws. It was this demand for symmetry or invariance in the description of nature that led Einstein first to the special and then to the general theory of relativity and that has apparently had a major role in shaping quantum theory.[1] The search for order

1. See Steven Weinberg, *Dreams of a Final Theory* (Pantheon Books, 1992), pp. 136–47. Bas van Fraassen in *Laws and Symmetry* (Oxford University Press, 1989) also emphasizes the role of symmetry in the formation of scientific theories, but his view is that their aim is only empirical adequacy, not the statement of objectively true laws of nature. Still, I take it he believes the empirically adequate theories we aim at are ones that *could* be objectively true.

and laws of nature seems from my amateur perspective to be driven by the broader idea that our local experiences and observations and the regularities we detect in them are manifestations of something else, something which includes us but on which none of us has a privileged perspective. Each of us is to think of our experiences as presenting us with an arbitrary or random sample of the universe.[2]

There are two potential charges of subjectivism with regard to this method. First, the demand for order cannot itself be rationally justified, nor does it correspond to a self-evident necessity, like arithmetic or logic. On a subjectivist view, the assumption of the uniformity of nature, on which science and ordinary empirical reasoning both depend, is simply the projection of our psychological need for a certain kind of world picture, rather than an intrinsically reliable tool for getting at the "mind-independent" truth.

Second, even the definition of what constitutes order seems to depend on us. For it means that at some level of description, similar causes will have similar effects on different occasions, and so forth—but the only measure of similarity we have available to us is what we count as similar, either by perception or by more technical methods of detection and measurement.[3] If that is so, then the method of arriving at factual conclusions by finding the best overall explanation or theory to account for the evidence is doubly subjective—first in its aim and second in what counts as success.

2. A fascinating discussion of these issues is found in Gerald Holton, "Mach, Einstein, and the Search for Reality," in his *Thematic Origins of Scientific Thought* (Harvard University Press, 1988). Einstein eventually rejected Mach's phenomenalism in favor of Planck's realism. Planck described the aim of science as "the complete liberation of the physical picture from the individuality of the separate intellects" (quoted in Holton, p. 245, from *Die Einheit des physikalischen Weltbildes*).

3. This is Nelson Goodman's "new" problem of induction. See *Fact, Fiction, and Forecast* (Harvard University Press, 1955; rprnt. Bobbs-Merrill, 1965).

I believe the only way to resist this charge is to argue that if those psychological analyses are taken seriously as hypotheses, they are themselves discredited by the very standards they purport to challenge. But can we make this argument without begging the question?

I think that we can and that there is an interesting difference in this respect between epistemological skepticism and the kind of subjectivism I wish to dispute. When G. E. Moore rebuts skepticism about the external world on the ground that he has two hands, he *is* begging the question; because if there are no material objects, then he doesn't have two hands, and he has done nothing to dispute the skeptic's argument either for the possibility that there are no material objects or for the impossibility of any evidence against its truth. A non-question-begging refutation would have to resist the skeptic en route to his conclusion.

In arguing against subjectivism, on the other hand, one is dealing not with a proposal of mere possibilities that cannot be excluded but with a positive interpretation of our thoughts. To gain acceptance, any such interpretation must survive in competition with other claims, and that includes the thoughts being interpreted, so long as they have not been displaced. If the subjectivist does not succeed in persuading us to suspend thinking the objective content of those thoughts, he has failed—just as the skeptic has failed if he does not cause us to doubt that we have hands. That is why I believe resistance to subjectivism can come from the content of objective thoughts themselves without necessarily begging the question. It is not question-begging, provided we rely on the thoughts themselves, rather than on the second-order claim that they must be interpreted objectively.

The subjectivist proposal is not that we don't know whether our beliefs about the world are correct but that it is a mistake to interpret them as beliefs about a mind-independent natural order. Rather, they should be understood as general features of our perspective or linguistic practice or point of view. My claim is that this is an alternative world picture—in which the central element is a set of human perspectives—and that it is in direct competition with the objective judgments it is meant to displace. Merely to propose this interpretation does not automatically make those judgments change their character. It produces instead a confrontation between two hypotheses: for example, the hypothesis that objects attract one another with a force directly proportional to the product of their masses and inversely proportional to the square of the distance between them, versus the hypothesis that it is a property of objects only as they appear to us (or in our language-game) that they attract each other with a force . . . , and so on. Unless the first hypothesis can be ruled out on some other grounds, it remains considerably more plausible than the second.

Confrontations between unqualified first-order claims and relativizing reinterpretations need not always result in victory for the former. Someone who has been brought up to believe that it is wrong for women to expose their breasts can come to realize at a certain point that this is a convention of his culture, and not an unqualified moral truth. Of course he *might* continue to insist, after examining the anthropological, historical, and sociological evidence, that it is wrong in itself for women to expose their breasts, and that cultures that fail to recognize the fact are in error. But this response is unlikely to survive the confrontation; it just doesn't have enough behind it (without, for example, a religious explanation of why exposure is wrong).

Unqualified judgments about astronomy, by contrast, are part of a world picture that is very robust in comparison with the Kantian alternative. Unless, as Kant thought, it is a picture that can be ruled out a priori, there is no reason why those judgments should not themselves weigh against a Kantian interpretation of them. In the same way, certain first-order moral judgments can resist emotivist interpretations by their own weight.

In each case we are presented with a conflict between two conceptions of the world and our place in it. Both conceptions are incomplete in various respects. There is no neutral standpoint from which they can be evaluated, so they have to compete with one another directly. The result may sometimes be a standoff, but it is not question-begging to regard the first-order credibility of a familiar proposition as a reason to reject a relativist or subjectivist interpretation of it. Of course one may be mistaken, but such mistakes are possible anywhere. (If two witnesses contradict each other, each maintaining that the other is lying, you can nevertheless conclude that the first is lying, on the basis of the testimony of the second; even if you are mistaken, you will not have begged the question.) There is no alternative to considering the alternatives and trying to make up one's mind.

III

One of the attractions of a subjectivist interpretation of empirical claims has always been that it would make radical skepticism impossible, because skepticism depends on interpreting the content of empirical claims—scientific or more ordinary—objectively, and then perceiving a logical gap between them and their empirical grounds. A recent example of subjectivism, usually presented as a way of transcending the outmoded subjective-objective distinction, is the view known as "internal realism," according to which our apparently objective world picture should be understood as essentially a creative product of our language and point of view, and the truth of our beliefs should be understood as their survival in an ideal development of that point of view. If, as Hilary Putnam has claimed, truth is nothing but "idealized rational acceptability,"[4] and if "acceptability" means "acceptability *to us*," then the logical gap between reasoning and the world disappears.

This position adds a qualification to our empirical claims that I believe is inconsistent with their content, in the same way that subjectivism about logic is inconsistent with its content. Furthermore, the only way to make literal sense of the qualification is in terms of a conception of the world and our place in it which is not itself subjective but according to which our entire system of substantive beliefs, by contrast, is. If we wish to adopt a view of the world that places our own thoughts within it and also answers to the demand for a natural order, it will have to be a view without such qualifications, subject to the same kind of reasoning about how things are that applies elsewhere—not a merely "internal" view.

Internal realism fails its own test of rational acceptability. What we in fact find rationally acceptable is a view of the world according to which we are located in it and arrive at beliefs about it that are confirmed and disconfirmed by our observations of what happens. Even if we concluded, as some physicists do about the quantum theory, that the best systematic account of what we observe cannot be given a realistic interpretation, that would still be a belief about how the world is, period—not a belief that it would be correct to qualify with an "internalist" reading. Reason is used to arrive at it, and the reasoning is not merely a development of our point of view, but objective thought about how things are.

More accurately, our point of view—what we accept on the basis of reason—*is* a set of beliefs about how things really are, together with copious acknowledgment that there is a lot

---

4. See *Reason, Truth and History* (Cambridge University Press, 1981). Putnam apparently held this view about mathematics and logic as well, but here I will restrict the discussion to empirical reason.

we don't know and perhaps a lot we can never know about how they really are. Here, just as in the case of logic and arithmetic, we can't get outside of our thoughts about what is the case and think of them *merely* as the expression of a point of view, within which their content must be situated. Their content, including the idea of a mind-independent reality, dominates any such self-conscious psychological or social image. One might put it as follows: There is no way of determining that a belief is rationally acceptable except by thinking about whether it is true—thinking about the evidence and the arguments and being open to consideration of whatever anyone brings up as relevant. To say that its truth *is* its rational acceptability deprives both the notion of truth and the notion of acceptability of all content.[5]

The belief that the world is orderly, and that our sense of

5. In *Representation and Reality* (MIT Press, 1988), Putnam asserts that internal realism is not supposed to be a reduction of truth to epistemic notions—that truth and rational acceptability are supposed to be interdependent (p. 115). But he doesn't make the position any clearer. On the other hand, still more recently, he seems to have edged away from the position, without actually saying so. Consider the following explanation of why Wittgenstein is not a relativist: "To say something is true in a language game is to stand outside of that language game and make a comment; that is not what it is to play a language game. Whatever it is that makes us want to replace moves like saying 'it's true' or 'it's reasonable' or 'it's warranted' by 'it's true in my language game' or 'it's reasonable in my language game' or 'it's warranted in my language game' (or makes us want to do this when we see that the language game itself is not grounded on Reason) is something that makes us want to *distance* ourselves from our own language game. It is as if the recognition that our language game does not have a transcendental justification made us want to handle it with kid gloves, or to handle it from a metalanguage. But why is the metalanguage any more secure?" (*Renewing Philosophy* [Harvard University Press, 1992], p. 176).

More recently still, in his Dewey Lectures, Putnam says, "Whether I am still, to some extent, an 'internal realist' is, I guess, as unclear as how much I was including under that unhappy label" (*Journal of Philosophy* 91 [1994], p. 463, n. 41).

what constitutes order (what properties are usable in the formulation of laws and inferences) is an indication of how the world is organized, is well confirmed in some areas, where we have discovered that the hypotheses to which we are led—theories about unobservables and the laws governing them—predict observations that are not themselves explainable by our belief in those hypotheses. The fact that observation is "theory-laden" seems to me an insignificant point which in no way tends to show that the process of confirming theories by observation is circular or nonobjective. It may require some theory, of telescopes or of photography, to interpret the astronomical photographs that show the bending of light rays by the sun's gravitational field, but the crucial observation—that the images of the stars near the sun are displaced outward—is not dependent on the theory which it confirms—namely, the general theory of relativity.

The possibility of noncircular confirmation is also, I think, the answer to doubts about the role of our natural sense of similarity in determining what counts for us as a regularity or law. The fact is that we can demote a similarity or a kind to the status of mere appearance, or similarity *for us,* only if it is shown to be not systematically connected with other observed regularities. But if some of the regularities we observe, including those revealed by measurement, turn out to be systematically correlated with others that emerge from different types of observation or measurement, then the most plausible hypothesis is that these are not artefacts of our perspective on the world but, rather, products of the world's systematic interaction with us. The scientific image of the physical world has in this way replaced the more associative and meaning-laden picture characteristic of earlier stages in the development of our culture. As a way of understanding inanimate nature, the latter method turns out to be circular, since the only "theories" it is capable of yielding are either mere summaries of the appearances or else delusional systems that give rise to appearances corresponding to them.[6]

Yet it has to be granted that the empirical confirmation of the supposition that the world is orderly and that particular phenomena can be explained by general laws has something inevitably circular about it. For when we formulate a law of some kind on the basis of our observations, and then confirm it by experiment, the confirmation, like the original formulation, depends on the judgment that the best systematic explanation of the relation between the original observations and the new experimental results is the one that relates them systematically—one according to which this is no accident. Someone who said at every point that the apparently law-confirming experimental results were just coincidence would be crazy, but he would not be contradicting himself. The idea of a law-governed world is not just the idea that there is a certain system among our actual observations but that this system can be explained by an order that governs the possibilities as well as the actualities and is not directly observable. We need to rely on the same general idea both to arrive at initial hypotheses about this order and to determine whether the hypotheses have been confirmed or disconfirmed.

But there is really no alternative. The attempt to reconstrue the ordered world picture as a projection of our minds founders on the need to place ourselves in the world so ordered. In trying to make sense of this relation, we are inevitably led to employ the same kind of reasoning, based on the search for order. Even if we decide that some of our apprehensions of order are illusions or errors, that will be because a better theory, by the same standards, can explain them away.

6. This description fits many of the applications of the term "theory" in postmodernist literary and cultural discourse.

Ultimately, all we can do is think about how the world is, including ourselves and our relation to the rest of it; and the only way to do that is to place our own experience in a larger setting that is suggested by the usual sort of empirical reasoning. It is certainly not a necessary truth that the world is orderly, let alone that we can understand its order. Substantial aspects of reality may never submit to this kind of intellectual grasp. But anything we can know about must be at least related in an orderly way to us, and an amazing amount has proved to be within our reach; given our achievements so far, it is reasonable to try to continue.

IV

The real problem is how to understand the inescapability of the idea of objective reality, which forces us to construe relativist or subjectivist interpretations of our thoughts as rival accounts of the world, in competition with the objectivist alternative. That is, it forces us, if we are asked to doubt the objectivity of our actual conceptions in some respect, to consider whether an alternative version of reality, known or unknown, is more likely to be true. A subjectivist interpretation of reason thus becomes just another hypothesis about the world and our relation to it, and that makes it subject finally to rational assessment, so that the aim of rational assessment of our beliefs turns out to be unavoidable. Subjectivism about human reason defeats itself, because it has to be evaluated as a hypothesis about our relation to the world.

This would not be necessary if a purely perspectival conception were an option—a conception in which the perspectives were not situated in any objective reality at all. But I believe it is not an option. Basically, I think that Descartes's *cogito* is correct. It is impossible to think of oneself except as something existing in the world—however little else the world may contain. But it is necessary to claim more than that, in order to counter the restriction on the scope of reason proposed by Kant.

Kant acknowledged that we could not help thinking of ourselves as part of an independently existing world, but he denied that reason or perception told us anything about how that world was in itself—not even about ourselves as parts of it. In fact, according to Kant, we can't even form a conception of what the world is like in itself, because every use of our capacity to reason, to form theories of objective reality, and to discover the best explanation of the appearances, is limited in its application to the phenomenal world—how things appear to us.

Although it is not strictly relativistic, since it grounds reason in a perspective that is universal for human beings, this is the most famous form of subjectivism about reason in the history of philosophy. If it were legitimate, it would block the application of the usual methods of reasoning about the world to itself: It would be exempt from the usual forms of assessment by which we evaluate a proposal about how things are. It is therefore important to question this status, since in a way it exemplifies the implied immunity from objective evaluation of all subjectivist views.

Kantian transcendental idealism is a thesis not about the phenomenal world but about the relation of the phenomenal world to the world as it is in itself. But since it says that ordinary scientific reasoning applies only to the phenomenal world, it exempts itself from the usual conditions of assessment. The thesis of transcendental idealism is not itself one of the synthetic a priori judgments whose validity it purports to explain, but it is an a priori claim all the same, based on the conviction that there is no other way things could be—that it is inconceivable that we should be able to use empirical evidence to find out about things as they are in themselves.

Now if this really is inconceivable, or self-contradictory, that is the end of the story. As Kant says, it implies that if spatial properties are supposed to belong to things in themselves, Berkeley's idealism is unavoidable.[7] But there is something fishy about insisting that we have the bare idea of our placement in a mind-independent world, while denying the logical possibility of anything more. I believe that once we admit this bare idea, we cannot exclude the possibility of forming hypotheses about that world. It then becomes necessary to interpret transcendental idealism itself as one of them—as the hypothesis that we know nothing whatever about those relations between us and the world that are responsible for the appearances.

I don't see how this proposal can be understood in a way that does not put it into competition with more mundane views about our place in the world and our relations with the rest of it, views that are supported by the ordinary methods of rational assessment and explanation. The Kantian position treats those methods as an aspect of the appearances for which no explanation is available to us, but why should that interpretation have priority over a straight reading? It is true that the two readings are mutually incompatible, so that if the Kantian view is correct, ordinary methods of reasoning cannot be used to evaluate it. On the other hand, if we stubbornly persist in trying to think about how things really are, then the Kantian view becomes just another hypothesis, unprotected from rational assessment and rejection.

I believe we cannot be dislodged from thinking about how things are, without qualification. Kant's admission of the bare idea of the noumenal world is actually an acknowledgment of this fact: We cannot make sense of transcendental idealism without it. But that bare concept is not enough to placate the demand for a conception of the world. To accept transcendental idealism we would have to cease to regard our ordinary

7. *Critique of Pure Reason*, B 274.

forms of thought as being about the world at all, and I think we cannot do that. We cannot be prevented from considering transcendental idealism as a minimalist theory of reality, which therefore forces us to consider whether it is true or not.

In thinking about the question, we are entitled to employ the forms of reasoning which the theory purports to disqualify as ways of determining what the world is really like—and we cannot avoid regarding them in precisely the way the theory forbids. We will ask whether this hypothesis is more plausible, on the evidence, than the alternatives. While it may remain as a skeptical possibility, not decisively refuted, it will not win automatically—and this means in effect that it will be refuted, since it is supposed to be not a mere possibility but a certainty.

Here, as elsewhere, reasoning in its own right defeats efforts to depict it as subordinate to something else that discredits its pretentions. It rears up its head to pass judgment on the very hypothesis that was designed to put it in its place. It inevitably reappears because any such hypothesis invites the question, "What reason do we have to think the world is really like that?" The alternatives always have to compete with the possibility that things are more or less as they appear to be—a possibility that can often be defeated, but only for reasons that make it less credible than one of the alternatives.

That makes it very difficult to dislodge the idea of a natural order and the associated search for regularities underlying what we observe. To the proposal that the order we appear to discover is just a framework we impose on experience, the inevitable, unexciting reply is that that does not seem a particularly likely explanation of the observed facts—that a more plausible account is that, to a considerable extent, the order that we find in our experience is the product of an order that is there independent of our minds. Applied to any real aspect of the natural order, the Kantian interpretation seems bizarre. For example, the detailed system of chemical laws summarized in the periodic table of the elements is not plausibly regarded as a result of the demands made on human experience by the conditions of the possibility of its having as objects things existing in time, either successively or simultaneously.[8]

This adverse judgment of course relies on precisely the kind of thought about the natural order that is being put in question, but it is unavoidable and therefore is not question-begging in a sense that would make the claim vacuous. The proposal that scientific reasoning tells us nothing about reality is itself a hypothesis about the world and cannot simply stop us from thinking, any more than a psychological reductionist theory of mathematics or ethics can stop us from thinking about arithmetic or right and wrong. There is no pure meta-level on which this argument can be carried out: The second-order theories cannot avoid competition with the content of what they are trying to reduce or debunk.

V

Once we leave behind the purely animal condition and reflect on our own impressions, we are faced with two possibilities. Either we can decide that they are correct, or at any rate worth retaining, or we can decide that they are in some respects erroneous and need to be altered. But in either case we can do this only from a newly developed conception of the world in which we are situated. We do not have the unintelligible option of reflecting on our antecedent conception of the world from some point of view that does not include a conception of the world. The outer frame of any view of ourselves, however

---

8. See the Analogies of Experience, in the *Critique of Pure Reason*. Kant holds that the extension of scientific theory to unobservables is also guided by the conditions of possible experience, since it describes what we would perceive if our senses were more refined. See his discussion of magnetism at B 273.

sophisticated and self-conscious, must consist of nonsubjective thoughts, taken straight. Nothing else is available, except completely empty nonsense—which is always available.

Upon placing ourselves in the world and regarding what we can observe as a sample of the whole, we may or may not discover an order that accounts for this sample in more universal terms. It is an important sign of the objectivity of the conception that our undeniable intellectual thirst for such order does not guarantee that it exists or that, if it exists, we can discover it by the combination of perception and thought. But when we do discover it, as has happened in various branches of natural science, the proposal that it is imposed by the conditions of our own experience, let alone by agreement, is completely implausible.

Something like that *can* happen, if experience is overwhelmingly influenced by an innate or acquired set of categories[9]—but when it does, that is a fact about the world that can be investigated by further thought and observation—a fact about the causation of certain appearances, rather than an a priori condition of their possibility. In the absence of reasons to believe in such a wrong-way influence, the supposition that the order we infer from our observations is an order of the real world in which we are contained becomes the natural one. It is subject to open-ended refinement, as we discover more and eliminate further distortions—but however we divide up the contributions of the external world and of our own perspective, the result is a conception of how the world is, ourselves included.

This is another example of the phenomenon of dominance, the dominance of general forms of empirical reasoning over any specific psychological or even metaphysical hypothesis about the explanation of such reasoning. Whatever is

9. Perhaps the long reign of Ptolemaic astronomy was an example.

proposed, we are entitled to ask—we cannot help asking—whether the proposal is supported by the evidence. Even if the proposal is specifically designed to provide a discrediting explanation of certain methods of drawing conclusions from the evidence, it cannot thereby exempt itself from assessment by those methods.

It is entirely possible that sometimes a challenge of this kind will succeed in destroying our confidence in certain methods of reasoning, with the result that those methods do not succeed in defeating the proposal even if they seem to dictate that it be rejected. But that will happen only if, in considering the proposal, we are convinced of its truth by other methods of reasoning that we are constrained to employ in their own right when faced with the argument and that provide us with something new to think.

I believe that Kant's transcendental idealism does not pass this test, because when we ask, contrary to its intent, whether on the basis of all the evidence it is a credible view of the world and of the nature of our knowledge of it, we find that our unrepentant empirical and scientific reasoning persists at full strength and does not reduce its realist claims in the face of this challenge. It continues to offer us good reasons in support of beliefs that are not merely about the phenomenal world, beliefs whose content directly contradicts what Kant has offered as an a priori analysis of the limitations of reason—and that defeat his analysis if they cannot be rationally dislodged.

It is not easy to explain the logical character of this opposition. Each party to the dispute is using precisely the methods that are being challenged by the other to refute the other's challenge, so it looks as though no one could possibly win. But that does not follow. Faced with such an apparent standoff, we just have to go on thinking about it and to decide which of the lines of reasoning is superior. The conclusion of the argument is to be found only in the arguments themselves that cannot be resisted—*not*, it should be noted, in the *fact* that they cannot

appearance

be resisted, but in their content. Kant's claim that empirical
reasoning tells us only about the phenomenal world is empirically incredible, given the evidence—and what is empirically
incredible is incredible, period.

Here, as elsewhere, a challenge to the universal claims of
reason has to propose an alternative that can be the object of
something like belief, or anyway acceptance; and none is available. There is nothing to appeal to, finally, when one is offering an idea for people's assent, except that they should think
about it; and thinking always leads, in the end, to reasoning
which at its outermost limits attempts to be universally valid
and to discover nonrelative truth. Try as we may, there is
nowhere to escape to from the pretensions of human reason.
— claims
If we try to reinterpret it in a more modest fashion, we find
ourselves, in carrying out the project, inevitably condemned
to forming beliefs of some kind about the world and our place
in it, and that can be done only by engaging in untrammeled
thought.

6

ETHICS

I

Let me now turn to the question of whether moral reasoning is also fundamental and inescapable. Unlike logical or arithmetical reasoning, it often fails to produce certainty, justified or unjustified. It is easily subject to distortion by morally irrelevant factors, social and personal, as well as outright error. It resembles empirical reason in not being reducible to a series of self-evident steps.

I take it for granted that the objectivity of moral reasoning does not depend on its having an external reference. There is no moral analogue of the external world—a universe of moral facts that impinge on us causally. Even if such a supposition made sense, it would not support the objectivity of moral reasoning. Science, which this kind of reifying realism takes as its model, doesn't derive its objective validity from the fact that it starts from perception and other causal relations between us and the physical world. The real work comes after that, in the form of active scientific reasoning, without which no amount of causal impact on us by the external world would generate a belief in Newton's or Maxwell's or Einstein's theories, or the chemical theory of elements and compounds, or molecular biology.

If we had rested content with the causal impact of the external world on us, we'd still be at the level of sense perception. We can regard our scientific beliefs as objectively true not because the external world causes us to have them but because we are able to *arrive at* those beliefs by methods that have a good claim to be reliable, by virtue of their success in selecting among rival hypotheses that survive the best criticisms and questions we can throw at them. Empirical confirmation plays a vital role in this process, but it cannot do so without theory.

Moral thought is concerned not with the description and explanation of what happens but with decisions and their justification. It is mainly because we have no comparably uncontroversial and well-developed methods for thinking about morality that a subjectivist position here is more credible than it is with regard to science. But just as there was no guarantee at the beginnings of cosmological and scientific speculation that we humans had the capacity to arrive at objective truth beyond the deliverances of sense-perception—that in pursuing it we were doing anything more than spinning collective fantasies—so there can be no decision in advance as to whether we are or are not talking about a real subject when we reflect and argue about morality. The answer must come from the results themselves. Only the effort to reason about morality can show us whether it is possible—whether, in thinking about what to do and how to live, we can find methods, reasons, and principles whose validity does not have to be subjectively or relativistically qualified.

Since moral reasoning is a species of practical reasoning, its conclusions are desires, intentions, and actions, or feelings and convictions that can motivate desire, intention, and action. We want to know how to live, and why, and we want the answer in general terms, if possible. Hume famously believed that because a 'passion' immune to rational assessment must underly every motive, there can be no such thing as specifically practical reason, nor specifically moral reason either. That is false, because while 'passions' are the source of some reasons, other passions or desires are themselves motivated and/or justified by reasons that do not depend on still more basic desires. And I would contend that either the question whether one should have a certain desire or the question whether, given that one has that desire, one should act on it, is always open to rational consideration.

The issue is whether the procedures of justification and criticism we employ in such reasoning, moral or merely practical, can be regarded finally as just something we do—a cultural or societal or even more broadly human collective practice, within which reasons come to an end. I believe that if we ask ourselves seriously how to respond to proposals for contextualization and relativistic detachment, they usually fail to convince. Although it is less clear than in some of the other areas we've discussed, attempts to get entirely outside of the object language of practical reasons, good and bad, right and wrong, and to see all such judgments as expressions of a contingent, nonobjective perspective will eventually collapse before the independent force of the first-order judgments themselves.

II

Suppose someone says, for example, "You only believe in equal opportunity because you are a product of Western liberal society. If you had been brought up in a caste society or one in which the possibilities for men and women were radically unequal, you wouldn't have the moral convictions you have or accept as persuasive the moral arguments you now accept." The second, hypothetical sentence is probably true, but what about the first—specifically the "only"? In general, the fact that I wouldn't believe something if I hadn't learned it proves nothing about the status of the belief or its grounds. It may be impossible to explain the learning without invoking the content of the belief itself, and the reasons for its truth; and it may be clear that what I have learned is such that even if I hadn't learned it, it would still be true. The reason the genetic fallacy is a fallacy is that the explanation of a belief can sometimes confirm it.

To have any content, a subjectivist position must say more

than that my moral convictions are my moral convictions. That, after all, is something we can all agree on. A meaningful subjectivism must say that they are *just* my moral convictions—or those of my moral community. It must *qualify* ordinary moral judgments in some way, must give them a self-consciously first-person (singular or plural) reading. That is the only type of antiobjectivist view that is worth arguing against or that it is even possible to disagree with.

But I believe it is impossible to come to rest with the observation that a belief in equality of opportunity, and a wish to diminish inherited inequalities, are merely expressions of our cultural tradition. True or false, those beliefs are essentially objective in intent. Perhaps they are wrong, but that too would be a nonrelative judgment. Faced with the fact that such values have gained currency only recently and not universally, one still has to try to decide whether they are right—whether one ought to continue to hold them. That question is not displaced by the information of contingency: The question remains, at the level of moral content, whether I would have been in error if I had accepted as natural, and therefore justified, the inequalities of a caste society, or a fairly rigid class system, or the orthodox subordination of women. It can take in additional facts as material for reflection, but the question of the relevance of those facts is inevitably a moral question: Do these cultural and historical variations and their causes tend to show that I and others have less reason than we had supposed to favor equality of opportunity? Presentation of an array of historically and culturally conditioned attitudes, including my own, does not disarm first-order moral judgment but simply gives it something more to work on—including information about influences on the formation of my convictions that may lead me to change them. But the relevance of such information is itself a matter for moral reasoning—about what are and are not good grounds for moral belief.

When one is faced with these real variations in practice

and conviction, the requirement to put oneself in everyone's shoes when assessing social institutions—some version of universalizability—does not lose any of its persuasive force just because it is not universally recognized. It dominates the historical and anthropological data: Presented with the description of a traditional caste society, I have to ask myself whether its hereditary inequalities are justified, and there is no plausible alternative to considering the interests of all in trying to answer the question. If others feel differently, they must say why they find these cultural facts relevant—why they require some qualification to the objective moral claim. On both sides, it is a moral issue, and the only way to defend universalizability or equal opportunity against subjectivist qualification is by continuing the moral argument. It is a matter of understanding exactly what the subjectivist wants us to give up, and then asking whether the grounds for those judgments disappear in light of his observations.

In my opinion, someone who abandons or qualifies his basic methods of moral reasoning on historical or anthropological grounds alone is nearly as irrational as someone who abandons a mathematical belief on other than mathematical grounds. Even with all their uncertainties and liability to controversy and distortion, moral considerations occupy a position in the system of human thought that makes it illegitimate to subordinate them completely to anything else. Particular moral claims are constantly being discredited for all kinds of reasons, but moral considerations per se keep rising again to challenge in their own right any blanket attempt to displace, defuse, or subjectivize them.

This is an instance of the more general truth that the normative cannot be transcended by the descriptive. The question "What should I do?" like the question "What should I believe?" is always in order. It is always possible to think about the question in normative terms, and the process is not rendered pointless by any fact of a different kind—any desire or emotion or feeling, any habit or practice or convention, any contingent cultural or social background. Such things may in fact guide our actions, but it is always possible to take their relation to action as an object of further normative reflection and ask, "How should I act, given that these things are true of me or of my situation?"

The type of thought that generates answers to this question is practical reason. But, further, it is always possible for the question to take a specifically moral form, since one of the successor questions to which it leads is, "What should anyone in my situation do?"—and consideration of that question leads in turn to questions about what everyone should do, not only in this situation but more generally.

Such universal questions don't always have to be raised, and there is good reason in general to develop a way of living that makes it usually unnecessary to raise them. But if they are raised, as they always can be, they require an answer of the appropriate kind—even though the answer may be that in a case like this one may do as one likes. They cannot be ruled out of order by pointing to something more fundamental—psychological, cultural, or biological—that brings the request for justification to an end. Only a justification can bring the request for justifications to an end. Normative questions in general are not undercut or rendered idle by anything, even though particular normative answers may be. (Even when some putative justification is exposed as a rationalization, that implies that something else could be said about the justifiability or nonjustifiability of what was done.)

III

The point of view to defeat, in a defense of the reality of practical and moral reason, is in essence the Humean one. Although Hume was wrong to say that reason was fit only to serve as the slave of the passions, it is nevertheless true that there are desires and sentiments prior to reason that it is not appropriate for reason to evaluate—that it must simply treat as part of the raw material on which its judgments operate. The question then arises how pervasive such brute motivational data are, and whether some of them cannot perhaps be identified as the true sources of those grounds of action which are usually described as reasons. Hume's theory of the "calm" passions was designed to make this extension, and resisting it is not a simple matter—even if it is set in the context of a minimal framework of practical rationality stronger than Hume would have admitted.

If there is such a thing as practical reason, it does not simply dictate particular actions but, rather, governs the *relations* among actions, desires, and beliefs—just as theoretical reason governs the relations among beliefs and requires some specific material to work on. Prudential rationality, requiring uniformity in the weight accorded to desires and interests situated at different times in one's life, is an example—and the example about which Hume's skepticism is most implausible, when he says it is not contrary to reason "to prefer even my own acknowledged lesser good to my greater, and have a more ardent affection for the former than the latter."[1] Yet Hume's position always seems a possibility, because whenever such a consistency requirement or similar pattern has an influence on our decisions, it seems possible to represent this influence as the manifestation of a systematic second-order desire or calm passion, which has such consistency as its object and without which we would not be susceptible to this type of "rational" motivation. Hume need then only claim that while such a desire (for the satisfaction of one's future interests) is

1. *A Treatise of Human Nature,* book 2, part 3, sec. 3 (L. A. Selby-Bigge, ed., Oxford University Press, 1888), p. 416. I'm afraid it's unavoidable to revisit the subject of prudence in a discussion of practical reason, overworked as it is.

quite common, to lack it is not contrary to reason, any more than to lack sexual desire is contrary to reason. The problem is to show how this misrepresents the facts.

The fundamental issue is about the order of explanation, for there is no point in denying that people have such second-order desires: the question is whether they are sources of motivation or simply the manifestation in our motives of the recognition of certain rational requirements. A parallel point could be made about theoretical reason. It is clear that the belief in modus ponens, for example, is not a rationally un-grounded *assumption* underlying our acceptance of deductive arguments that depend on modus ponens: Rather, it is simply a recognition of the validity of that form of argument.[2]

The question is whether something similar can be said of the "desire" for prudential consistency in the treatment of desires and interests located at different times. I think it can be and that if one tries instead to regard prudence as simply a desire among others, a desire one happens to have, the question of its appropriateness inevitably reappears as a normative question, and the answer can only be given in terms of the principle itself. The normative can't be displaced by the psychological.

If I think, for example, "What if I didn't care about what would happen to me in the future?" the appropriate reaction is not like what it would be to the supposition that I might not care about movies. True, I'd be missing something if I didn't care about movies, but there are many forms of art and entertainment, and we don't have to consume them all. Note that even this is a judgment of the *rational acceptability* of such

2. See Barry Stroud, "Inference, Belief, and Understanding," *Mind* 88 (1979), p. 187: "For every proposition or set of propositions the belief or acceptance of which is involved in someone's believing one proposition on the basis of another there must be something else, not simply a further proposition accepted, that is responsible for the one belief's being based on the other."

variation—of there being no reason to regret it. The supposition that I might not care about my own future cannot be regarded with similar tolerance: It is the supposition of a real failure—the paradigm of something to be regretted—and my recognition of that failure does not reflect merely the antecedent presence in me of a contingent second-order desire. Rather, it reflects a judgment about what is and what is not relevant to the justification of action against a certain factual background.

Relevance and consistency both get a foothold when we adopt the standpoint of decision, based on the total circumstances, including our own condition. This standpoint introduces a subtle but profound gap between desire and action, into which the free exercise of reason enters. It forces us to the idea of the difference between doing the right thing and doing the wrong thing (here, without any specifically ethical meaning as yet)—given our total situation, *including* our desires. Once I see myself as the subject of certain desires, as well as the occupant of an objective situation, I still have to decide what to do, and that will include deciding what justificatory weight to give to those desires.

This step back, this opening of a slight space between inclination and decision, is the condition that permits the operation of reason with respect to belief as well as with respect to action, and that poses the demand for generalizable justification. The two kinds of reasoning are in this way parallel. It is only when, instead of simply being pushed along by impressions, memories, impulses, desires, or whatever, one stops to ask "What should I do?" or "What should I believe?" that reasoning becomes possible—and, having become possible, becomes necessary. Having stopped the direct operation of impulse by interposing the possibility of decision, one can get one's beliefs and actions into motion again only by thinking about what, in light of the circumstances, one should do.

The controversial but crucial point, here as everywhere in

the discussion of this subject, is that the standpoint from which one assesses one's choices after this step back is not just first-personal. One is suddenly in the position of judging what one ought to do, against the background of all one's desires and beliefs, in a way that does not merely flow from those desires and beliefs but *operates* on them—by an assessment that should enable anyone else also to see what is the right thing for you to do against that background.

It is not enough to find some higher order desires that one happens to have, to settle the matter: such desires would have to be placed among the background conditions of decision along with everything else. Rather, even in the case of a purely self-interested choice, one is seeking the right answer. One is trying to decide what, given the inner and outer circumstances, *one should do*—and that means not just what *I* should do but what *this person* should do. The same answer should be given to that question by anyone to whom the data are presented, whether or not he is in your circumstances and shares your desires. That is what gives practical reason its generality.

The objection that has to be answered, here as elsewhere, is that this sense of unconditioned, nonrelative judgment is an illusion—that we cannot, merely by stepping back and taking ourselves as objects of contemplation, find a secure platform from which such judgment is possible. On this view whatever we do, after engaging in such an intellectual ritual, will still inevitably be a manifestation of our individual or social nature, not the deliverance of impersonal reason—for there is no such thing.

But I do not believe that such a conclusion can be established a priori, and there is little reason to believe it could be established empirically. The subjectivist would have to show that all purportedly rational judgments about what people have reason to do are really expressions of rationally unmotivated desires or dispositions of the person making the judgment—desires or dispositions to which normative assessment has no application. The motivational explanation would have to have the effect of *displacing* the normative one—showing it to be superficial and deceptive. It would be necessary to make out the case about many actual judgments of this kind and to offer reasons to believe that something similar was true in all cases. Subjectivism involves a positive claim of empirical psychology.

Is it conceivable that such an argument could succeed? In a sense, it would have to be shown that all our supposed practical reasoning is, at the limit, a form of rationalization. But the defender of practical reason has a general response to all psychological claims of this type. Even when some of his actual reasonings are convincingly analyzed away as the expression of merely parochial or personal inclinations, it will in general be reasonable for him to add this new information to the body of his beliefs about himself and then step back once more and ask, "What, in light of all this, do I have reason to do?" It is logically conceivable that the subjectivist's strategy might succeed by exhaustion; the rationalist might become so discouraged at the prospect of being once again undermined in his rational pretensions that he would give up trying to answer the recurrent normative question. But it is far more likely that the question will always be there, continuing to appear significant and to demand an answer. To give up would be nothing but moral laziness.

More important, as a matter of substance I do not think the subjectivist's project can be plausibly carried out. It is not possible to give a debunking psychological explanation of prudential rationality, at any rate. For suppose it is said, plausibly enough, that the disposition to provide for the future has survival value and that its implantation in us is the product of natural selection. As with any other instinct, we still have to decide whether acting on it is a good idea. With some biologically natural dispositions, both motivational and intellectual, there are good reasons to resist or limit their influence. That this does not seem the right reaction to prudential motives (except insofar as we limit them for moral reasons) shows that they cannot be regarded simply as desires that there is no reason to have. If they were, they wouldn't give us the kind of reasons for action that they clearly do.[3] It will never be reasonable for the rationalist to concede that prudence is just a type of consistency in action that he happens, groundlessly, to care about, and that he would have no reason to care about if he didn't already.

The null hypothesis—that in this unconditional sense there are no reasons—is acceptable only if from the point of view of detached self-observation it is superior to the alternatives; and as elsewhere, I believe it fails that test.

IV

Bernard Williams is a prominent contemporary representative of the opposite view. In chapter 4 of *Ethics and the Limits of Philosophy*,[4] he argues that reflective practical reason, unlike reflective theoretical reason, always remains first-personal: One is always trying to answer the question "What shall (or should) *I* do?" and the answer must derive from something internal to what he calls one's "motivational set." Williams says that in theoretical reasoning, by contrast, while it is true that one is trying to decide what to believe, the question "What should I believe?" is in general replaceable by a substantive question which need make no first-person reference: a question like "Did Wagner ever meet Verdi?" or "Is strontium a metal?" This means that the pursuit of freedom through the rational, reflective assessment of the influences on one's be-

3. For a very persuasive argument that brute desires or preferences in themselves *never* provide reasons for action, see Warren Quinn, "Putting Rationality in Its Place," in his *Morality and Action* (Cambridge University Press, 1993).

4. Harvard University Press, 1985.

liefs leads, in the theoretical case, to the employment of objective, non-first-personal standards. To decide what to believe, I have to decide, in light of the evidence available to me, and by standards that it would be valid for anyone to use in drawing a conclusion from that evidence, what is probably true.

But Williams holds that in deciding what to do, even if I try to free myself from the blind pressures of my desires and instincts by reflecting on those influences and evaluating their suitability as reasons for action, such reflection will never take me outside of the domain of first-personal thought. Even at my most reflective, it will still be a decision about what *I* should do and will have to be based on *my* reflective assessment of my motives and reasons. To believe that at some point I will reach a level of reflection where I can consider truly objective reasons, valid for anyone, that reveal what *should be done* by this person in these circumstances, is to deceive myself. In the practical domain, there is no such standpoint of assessment.[5]

It has to be admitted that phenomenologically, the subjectivist view is more plausible in ethics than in regard to theoretical reason. When I step back from my practical reasonings and ask whether I can endorse them as correct, it is possible to experience this as a move to a deeper region of myself rather than to a higher universal standpoint. Yet at the same time there seems to be no limit to the possibility of asking whether the first-personal reasoning I rely on in deciding what to do is also objectively acceptable. It always seems appropriate to ask, setting aside that the person in question is oneself, "What ought to happen? What is the right thing to do, in this case?"

That the question can take this form does not follow merely from the fact that it is always possible to step back from

5. Actually, there is a bit of obscurity in Williams's view on this point, since he may believe there is an objective answer, discoverable by anyone, to the question of what a particular person should do, given the contents of his "motivational set." See the essay "Internal and External Reasons" in his collection *Moral Luck* (Cambridge University Press, 1981), pp. 103–5.

one's present intentions and motives and consider whether one wishes to change them. The fact that the question "What should I do?" is always open, or reopenable, is logically consistent with the answer's always being a first-personal answer. It might be, as Williams believes, that the highest freedom I can hope for is to ascend to higher order desires or values that are still irreducibly my own—values that determine what kind of person I as an individual wish to be—and that all apparently objective answers to the question are really just the first person masquerading as the third. But do values really disappear into thin air when we adopt the external point of view? Since we can reach a *descriptive* standpoint from which the first person has vanished and from which one regards oneself impersonally, the issue is whether at that point description outruns evaluation. If it does not, if evaluation of some sort keeps pace with it, then we will finally have to evaluate our conduct from a non-first-person standpoint.

Clearly, description can outrun some evaluations. If I don't like shrimp, there simply is no higher order evaluation to be made of this preference. All I can do is to observe that I have it; and no higher order value seems to be involved when it leads me to refrain from ordering a dish containing shrimp or to decline an offer of shrimp when the hors d'oeuvres are passed at a cocktail party. However external a view I may take of the preference, I am not called on either to defend it or to endorse it: I can just accept it. But there are other evaluations, by contrast, that seem at least potentially to be called into question by an external, descriptive view, and the issue is whether those questions always lead us finally to a first-person answer.

Suppose I reflect on my political preferences—my hope that candidate X will not win the next presidential election, for example. What external description of this preference, considered as a psychological state, is consistent with its stability? Can I regard my reasons for holding it simply as facts about myself, as my dislike of shrimp is a fact about myself? Or will any purely descriptive observation of such facts give rise to a further evaluative question—one that cannot be answered simply by a reaffirmation that this is the kind of person I am?

Here, as elsewhere, I don't think we can hope for a decisive proof that we are asking objective questions and pursuing objective answers. The possibility that we are deceiving ourselves is genuine. But the only way to deal with that possibility is to think about it, and one must think about it by weighing the plausibility of the debunking explanation against the plausibility of the ethical reasoning at which it is aimed. The claim that, at the most objective level, the question of what we should do becomes meaningless has to compete head-to-head with specific claims about what in fact we should do, and their grounds. So in the end, the contest is between the credibility of substantive ethics and the credibility of an external psychological reduction of that activity.

V   FREEDOM

There is a deep philosophical problem about the capacity to step back and evaluate either one's actions or one's beliefs; it is the problem of free will.

Suppose you became convinced that *all* your choices, decisions, and conclusions were determined by rationally arbitrary features of your psychological makeup or by external manipulation, and then tried to ask yourself what, in the light of this information, you should do or believe. There would really be no way to answer the question, because the arbitrary causal control of which you had become convinced would apply to whatever you said or decided.[6] You could not simultaneously believe this about yourself and try to make a free, rational choice. Not only that, but if the very belief in the causal system of control was itself a product of what you thought to be reasoning, then it too would lose its status as a belief freely

6. Recall the scrambled-brain hypothesis in chapter 4.

arrived at, and your attitude toward it would have to change.
(Though even *that* is a rational argument, whose conclusion
you are no longer in a position to draw!)

Doubt about your own rationality is unstable; it leaves you
really with nothing to think. So although the hypothesis of
nonrational control seems a contingent possibility, it is no
more possible to entertain it with regard to yourself than it is
to consider the possibility that you are not thinking. I have
never known how to respond to this conundrum.

However, a more specialized version of the problem can
be raised about practical reason alone. The hypothesis that
practical reason does not exist is not self-contradictory. In
spite of everything I have said, one might intelligibly suppose,
without having to abandon *all* one's reasoning, that decisions
to act are all ultimately due to arbitrary desires and dispositions—perhaps higher order and partly unconscious—that
lie beyond the possibility of rational assessment. Consider the
hypothesis that this is true in particular whenever we take
ourselves to be engaged in practical reasoning. If someone
actually believed this, he could not ask, "In light of all that,
what should I do?" To ask that, hoping for a genuinely rational evaluation of the alternatives, would contradict the supposition of nonrational determination, which is supposed to apply to all choices, including this one. So if one really accepted
the hypothesis, one would have to abandon the practice of
rational assessment, all things considered, as an illusion, and
limit the practical employment of reason to an instrumental
role.

But is that possible? I don't think so; rather, I think the
illusion is on the other side, in trying to see oneself as nonra-
tionally determined. What we have here is a face-off between
two attitudes—not, as in the case of subjectivism about theoretical reason, between two theories about how things are.
The opposition here is between a theory about how things are
and a practice that would be impossible if this was how things

were. If we go on trying to make up our minds about what to do on the basis of the best reasons, we implicitly reject the hypothesis of an ultimately nonrational determination of what we do. (I leave open the possibility that there is a form of causal determination that is compatible with rationality; if so, we could simultaneously engage in practical and theoretical reasoning and believe that we were so determined—including being so determined to believe that we were.)

The unquenchable persistence of the conviction that it is up to me to decide, all things considered, what I should do, is what Kant called the *fact of reason*.[7] It reveals itself in decision, not in contemplation—in the permanent capacity we have to contemplate all the personal, contingent features of our motivational circumstances and ask, once again, "What should I do?"—and in our persistent attempts to answer the question, even if it is very difficult. The sense of freedom depends on the decision's not being merely from *my* point of view. It is not just a working out of the implications of my own perspective, but the demand that my actions conform to universally applicable standards that make them potentially part of a harmonious collective system. Thus I find within myself the universal standards that enable me to get outside of myself. (In Kant's example, I am directly aware of the fact of reason when the tyrant threatens to kill me unless I bear false witness against an innocent man: I know that I *can* refuse—whether or not I will be brave enough to do so—because I know that I *ought* to refuse.)[8]

There is a direct analogy here with the operation of theoretical reason, which employs universal principles of belief formation to bring my thoughts into harmony with a consis-

---

7. *Critique of Practical Reason* (trans. Lewis White Beck, Bobbs-Merrill, 1956), original in vol. 5 of the Prussian Academy edition of Kant's works, pp. 31, 42.
8. *Critique of Practical Reason*, pp. 30, 155–9.

tent system of objective beliefs in which others can also hold a share—more commonly known as *the truth*. Reason is an attempt to turn myself into a local representative of the truth, and in action of the right. Freedom requires holding oneself in one's hands and choosing a direction in thought or action for the highly contingent and particular individual that one is, from a point of view outside oneself, that one can nevertheless reach from inside oneself.

This picture is opposed to the Humean alternative which limits reason to thought and gives it no direct application to conduct. According to that view, we may transcend ourselves to develop a truer and more objective conception of how the world is, but this transcendence influences our conduct only instrumentally—by revealing how we may most effectively act on our motives, which remain entirely perspectival. Even where an objective view of the facts leads us to pursue practical harmony with others, the motives remain personal.

But I believe that alternative is untenable. Even a moral system like that of Hobbes, based on the rational construction of collective self-interest, affirms the rationality of the self-interest on which it depends. And that puts it in competition with other conceptions of what is rational.

We cannot evade our freedom. Once we have developed the capacity to recognize our own desires and motives, we are faced with the choice of whether to act as they incline us to act, and in facing that choice we are inevitably faced with an evaluative question. Even if we refuse to think about it, that refusal can itself be evaluated. In this sense I believe Kant was right: The applicability to us of moral concepts is the consequence of our freedom—freedom that comes from the ability to see ourselves objectively, through the new choices which that ability forces on us.[9]

---

9. For an illuminating treatment of this subject, see Christine Korsgaard, *The Sources of Normativity* (Cambridge University Press, 1996).

VI

Even a 'subjective'-seeming solution to this problem—like the answer that there are no universal standards for determining what we should do, and that each person may follow his own inclinations—is itself an objective, universal claim and therefore a limiting case of a moral position. But that position obviously has competitors, and one or another of the moralities that require some kind of impartial consideration for everyone is much more plausible. Let me now sketch out in a series of rough steps the familiar kinds of substantive practical reasoning that lead to this conclusion and that resist a Humean reduction.

The first step on the path to ethics is the admission of *generality* in practical judgments. That is actually equivalent to the admission of the existence of reasons, for a reason is something one person can have only if others would also have it if they were in the same circumstances (internal as well as external). In taking an objective view of myself, the first question to answer is whether I have, in this generalizable sense, any reason to do anything, and a negative answer is nearly as implausible as a negative answer to the analogous question of whether I have any reason to believe anything. Neither of those questions—though they are, to begin with, about me—is essentially first-personal, since they are supposed not to depend for their answers on the fact that I am asking them.

It is perhaps less impossible to answer the question about practical reasons in the negative than the question about theoretical reasons. (And by a negative answer, remember, we mean the position that there *are* no reasons, not merely that I have no reason to believe, or do, anything rather than anything else—the skeptical position, which is also universal in its grounds and implications.) If one ceased to recognize theoretical reasons, having reached a reflective standpoint, it would make no sense to go on having beliefs, though one might be unable to stop. But perhaps action wouldn't likewise become senseless if one denied the existence of practical reasons: One could still be moved by impulse and habit, without thinking that what one did was justified in any sense—even by one's inclinations—in a way that admitted generalization.

However, this seems a very implausible option. It implies, for example, that none of your desires and aversions, pleasures and sufferings, or your survival or death, give you any generalizable reason to do anything—that all we can do from an objective standpoint is to observe, and perhaps try to predict, what you *will* do. The application of this view to my own case is outlandish: I can't seriously believe that I have *no reason* to get out of the way of a truck that is bearing down on me in the street—that my motive is a purely psychological reaction not subject to rational endorsement. Clearly I have a reason, and clearly it is generalizable.

The second step on the path to familiar moral territory is the big one: the choice between agent-relative, essentially egoistic (but still general) reasons and some alternative that admits agent-neutral reasons[10] or in some other way acknowledges that each person has a noninstrumental reason to consider the interests of others. It is possible to understand this choice partly as a choice of the way in which one is going to value oneself and one's own interests. It has strong implications in that regard.

Morality is possible only for beings capable of seeing themselves as one individual among others more or less similar in general respects—capable, in other words, of seeing themselves as others see them. When we recognize that although we occupy only our own point of view and not that of anyone else, there is nothing cosmically unique about it, we are faced with a choice. This choice has to do with the relation

10. For this terminology, see *The View from Nowhere* (Oxford University Press, 1986), pp. 152-3.

between the value we naturally accord to ourselves and our fates from our own point of view, and the attitude we take toward these same things when viewed from the impersonal standpoint that assigns to us no unique status apart from anyone else.

One alternative would be not to "transfer" to the impersonal standpoint in any form those values which concern us from the personal standpoint. That would mean that the impersonal standpoint would remain purely descriptive and our lives and what matters to us as we live them (including the lives of other people we care about) would not be regarded as mattering at all if considered apart from the fact that they are ours, or personally related to us. Each of us, then, would have a system of values centering on his own perspective and would recognize that others were in exactly the same situation.

The other alternative would be to assign to one's life and what goes on in it some form of impersonal as well as purely perspectival value, not dependent on its being one's own. This would then imply that everyone else was also the subject of impersonal value of a similar kind.

The agent-relative position that all of a person's reasons derive from his own interests, desires, and attachments means that I have no reason to care about what happens to other people unless what happens to them matters to me, either directly or instrumentally. This is compatible with the existence of strong derivative reasons for consideration of others—reasons for accepting systems of general rights, and so forth—but it does not include those reasons at the ground level. It also means, of course, that others have no reason to care about what happens to me—again, unless it matters to them in some way, emotionally or instrumentally. All the practical reasons that any of us have, on this theory, depend on what is valuable *to us*.

It follows that we each have value only to ourselves and to those who care about us. Considered impersonally, we are valueless and provide no intrinsic reasons for concern to anyone. So the egoistic answer to the question of what kinds of reasons there are amounts to an assessment of oneself, along with everyone else, as *objectively worthless*. In a sense, it doesn't matter (except to ourselves) what happens to us: Each person has value only *for himself*, not *in himself*.

Now this judgment, while it satisfies the generality condition for reasons, and while perfectly consistent, is in my opinion highly unreasonable and difficult to honestly accept. Can you really believe that objectively, it doesn't matter whether you die of thirst or not—and that your inclination to believe that it does is just the false objectification of your self-love? One could really ask the same question about anybody else's dying of thirst, but concentrating on your own case stimulates the imagination, which is why the fundamental moral argument takes the form, "How would you like it if someone did that to you?" The concept of reasons for action faces us with a question about their content that it is very difficult to answer in a consistently egoistic or agent-relative style.

VII

This step takes us to the basic platform of other-regarding moral thought, but at that point the path forward becomes more difficult to discern. We may admit that a system of reasons should accord to persons and their interests some kind of objective, as well as subjective, worth, but there is more than one way to do this, and none of them is clearly the right one; no doubt there are other ways, not yet invented, which are superior to those that have been. As a final illustration of the attempt to discover objective practical reasons, let me discuss the familiar contrast between two broad approaches to the interpretation of objective worth, represented by utilitarian and contractualist (or rights-based) moral theories, respectively. This is also, I must admit, the type of case where skepticism about the objectivity of reasons is most plausible, precisely because the substantive arguments are not decisive.

The problem is to give more specific content to the idea that persons have value not just *for* themselves but *in* themselves—and therefore for everyone. That means we all have some kind of reason to consider one another, but what kind is it? What is the right way to think from an objective standpoint about the nonegoistic system of reasons generated by multiple individual lives?

Each of the two approaches answers the question in a way that attempts to give equal value to everyone; the difference between them lies in the kind of equality they endorse. Utilitarianism assigns equal value to people's actual experiences, positive and negative: Everyone's personal good *counts* the same, as something to be advanced. The equal moral value that utilitarianism assigns to everyone is equality as a *component* of the totality of value. This leads to the characteristic aggregative and maximizing properties of utilitarian moral reasoning. Everyone is treated equally as a source of inputs to the calculation of value, but once that is done, it is total value rather than equality that takes over as the goal. Utilitarianism may have problems supplying a usable common measure of well-being for combinatorial purposes, but it is certainly a viable method of moral reasoning. If it is taken as the whole truth about morality, then rights, obligations, equality, and other deontological elements have to be explained derivatively, on the ground of their instrumental value in promoting the greatest overall good for people in the long run. The rule-utilitarian treatment of those topics is well developed and familiar.

The other approach is associated with the social contract tradition and Kant's categorical imperative. It accords to everyone not equality of input into the totality of value, but equality of status and treatment in certain respects. The way it acknowledges everyone's objective value is to offer certain universal substantive guarantees—protections against violation and provision of basic needs. Equality in moral status is therefore much closer to the surface of contractualist than of utilitarian moral recognition. Contractualism uses a system of priorities rather than maximization of total well-being as the method of settling conflicts between interests. It also allows the admission of rights, obligations, and distributive equality as fundamental features of the system of moral reasons rather than as derivative features justified only by their instrumental value. The resulting system will include certain guaranteed protections to everyone, in the form of individual rights against interference, as well as priority in the provision of benefits to serve the most urgent needs, which are in general to be met before less urgent interests, even of larger numbers of persons, are addressed.

The dispute between a priority or rights-based theory and a maximizing, aggregative theory is really a disagreement over the best way to interpret the extremely general requirement of impartial interpersonal concern.[11] The issue is at the moment highly salient and controversial, and I do not propose to take it further here. I introduce it only as an example of a large substantive question of moral theory, one that firmly resists subjectivist or relativist interpretation: The question demands that we look for the right answer rather than relying on our feelings or the consensus of our community.

Once we admit the existence of some form of other-regarding reasons that are general in application, we have to look for a way of specifying their content and principles of combination. That is not a first-person enterprise. We are trying to decide what reasons there are, having already decided that there must be *some*, in a certain broad category—a

11. For an alternative position see Christine Korsgaard's essay "The Reasons We Can Share: An Attack on the Distinction between Agent-relative and Agent-neutral Values," *Social Philosophy and Policy* 10, no. 1 (1993).

generally applicable way of answering the question "What is the right thing to do in these circumstances?" That is simply a continuation of the original task of objective judgment that faced us when we took the first reflective step, by asking whether, from an impersonal point of view, we have any reasons to do anything at all. To answer the question it is not enough to consult my own inclinations; I have to try to arrive at a judgment. Such judgments often take the form of moral intuitions, but those are not just subjective reactions, at least in intention: They are beliefs about what is right.

The situation here is like that in any other basic domain. First-order thoughts about its content—thoughts expressed in the object language—rise up again as the decisive factor in response to all second-order thoughts about their psychological character. They look back at the observer, so to speak. And those first-order thoughts aim to be valid without qualification, however much pluralism or even relativism may appear as part of their (objective) content. It is in that sense that ethics is one of the provinces of reason, if it is. That is why we can defend moral reason only by abandoning metatheory for substantive ethics. Only the intrinsic weight of first-order moral thinking can counter the doubts of subjectivism. (And the less its weight, the more plausible subjectivism becomes.)[12]

---

12. For Ronald Dworkin's closely related treatment of these issues, see his essay "Objectivity and Truth: You'd Better Believe It," *Philosophy & Public Affairs* 25, no. 2 (1996).

7

EVOLUTIONARY NATURALISM
AND THE FEAR OF RELIGION

I

Charles Sanders Peirce is usually described as the founder
of pragmatism, but that is no more accurate than describing
Wittgenstein as the founder of logical positivism. Wittgenstein's account in the *Tractatus* of significant propositions was
transformed by the positivists into a theory of everything,
though he himself declared that what couldn't in this sense be
said was much more important than what could be. Similarly,
it appears, Peirce's account of the appropriate grounds of
belief was transformed by the pragmatists into a general theory of truth, even though Peirce thought belief of merely
practical significance and held that mere belief had no place in
science—which, on the contrary, was to be guided by reason
and cognitive instinct. Here is a quotation from a wonderful,
relatively late work of his:

> We *believe* the proposition we are ready to act upon. *Full
> belief* is willingness to act upon the proposition in vital crises,
> *opinion* is willingness to act upon it in relatively insignificant
> affairs. But pure science has nothing at all to do with *action*.
> The propositions it accepts, it merely writes in the list of
> premises it proposes to use.[1]

1. Peirce, *Reasoning and the Logic of Things*, edited by Kenneth Laine
Ketner, with introduction and commentary by Ketner and Hilary Putnam
(Harvard University Press, 1992), p. 112. It is the text of eight lectures deliv-
ered in Cambridge, Massachusetts, in 1898.

In science, the correct method is to avoid becoming attached to any propositions in the manner of belief (I find this use of the word "belief" somewhat peculiar, but the point is clear), however necessary that may be for practical affairs. The only way we can have any hope of advancing toward the truth is to be continually dissatisfied with our opinions, to be always on the lookout for objections, and to be prepared to drop or alter our theories whenever counterevidence, counterarguments, or better-supported alternatives present themselves. Only the willingness to change one's mind gives any ground for thinking that what one hasn't been persuaded to change one's mind about may be right, or at least on the right track.

But if not belief, in the sense of what one is prepared to act on, what is the proper aim of science, according to Peirce? Far from being a pragmatist in the currently accepted sense, he seems much more of a Platonist:

> Belief is the willingness to risk a great deal upon a proposition. But this belief is no concern of science which has nothing at stake on any temporal venture, but is in pursuit of eternal verities, not semblances to truth, and looks upon this pursuit, not as the work of one man's life, but as that of generation after generation indefinitely.[2]

Here we may have some indication of the familiar Peircian idea of convergence at the end of inquiry, but if so, it is certainly not presented as a *definition* of truth, but as a hope that rational inquiry will lead us to truths that depend not on our minds but on nature:

> The only end of science, as such, is to learn the lesson that the universe has to teach it. In Induction it simply surrenders itself to the force of facts. But it finds . . . that this is not enough. It is driven in desperation to call upon its inward sympathy with nature, its instinct for aid, just as we

2. Ibid., p. 177.

find Galileo at the dawn of modern science making his appeal to *il lume naturale*. . . . The value of *Facts to it*, lies only in this, that they belong to Nature; and nature is something great, and beautiful, and sacred, and eternal, and real,—the object of its worship and its aspiration.[3]

And one final Platonic morsel:

The soul's deeper parts can only be reached through its surface. In this way the eternal forms, that mathematics and philosophy and the other sciences make us acquainted with will by slow percolation gradually reach the very core of one's being, and will come to influence our lives; and this they will do, not because they involve truths of merely vital importance, but because they [are] ideal and eternal verities.[4]

Now I find these declarations not only eloquent but entirely congenial; but they have a radically antireductionist and realist tendency quite out of keeping with present fashion. And they are alarmingly Platonist in that they maintain that the project of pure inquiry[5] is sustained by our "inward sympathy" with nature, on which we draw in forming hypotheses that can then be tested against the facts. Something similar must be true of reason itself, which according to Peirce has nothing to do with "how we think."[6] If we can reason, it is because our thoughts can obey the order of the logical relations among propositions—so here again we depend on a Platonic harmony.

The reason I call this view alarming is that it is hard to know what world picture to associate it with, and difficult to

3. Ibid., pp. 176–7.
4. Ibid., pp. 121–2. Unhappily, while writing the lectures Peirce had been urged by William James to concentrate less on logic and consider instead addressing "separate topics of a vitally important character." (See the introduction, p. 25.)
5. This is Bernard Williams's name for the Cartesian project of trying to discover the truth, without regard to any practical considerations whatever; see his *Descartes: the Project of Pure Inquiry* (Penguin, 1978).
6. *Reasoning and the Logic of Things*, p. 143.

avoid the suspicion that the picture will be religious, or quasi-religious. Rationalism has always had a more religious flavor than empiricism. Even without God, the idea of a natural sympathy between the deepest truths of nature and the deepest layers of the human mind, which can be exploited to allow gradual development of a truer and truer conception of reality, makes us more *at home* in the universe than is secularly comfortable.[7] The thought that the relation between mind and the world is something fundamental makes many people in this day and age nervous. I believe this is one manifestation of a fear of religion which has large and often pernicious consequences for modern intellectual life.

In speaking of the fear of religion, I don't mean to refer to the entirely reasonable hostility toward certain established religions and religious institutions, in virtue of their objectionable moral doctrines, social policies, and political influence. Nor am I referring to the association of many religious beliefs with superstition and the acceptance of evident empirical falsehoods. I am talking about something much deeper—namely, the fear of religion itself. I speak from experience, being strongly subject to this fear myself: I want atheism to be true and am made uneasy by the fact that some of the most intelligent and well-informed people I know are religious believers. It isn't just that I don't believe in God and, naturally, hope that I'm right in my belief. It's that I hope there is no God! I don't want there to be a God; I don't want the universe to be like that.[8]

---

7. To a lesser degree, the same might be said of the idea of human access to values that are objective or universal.

8. I won't attempt to speculate about the Oedipal and other sources of either this desire or its opposite. (About the latter there has already been considerable speculation—Freud's *The Future of an Illusion,* for example.) I am curious, however, whether there is anyone who is genuinely indifferent as to whether there is a God—anyone who, whatever his actual belief about the matter, doesn't particularly *want* either one of the answers to be correct (though of course he might want to *know* which answer was correct).

My guess is that this cosmic authority problem is not a rare condition and that it is responsible for much of the scientism and reductionism of our time.[9] One of the tendencies it supports is the ludicrous overuse of evolutionary biology to explain everything about life, including everything about the human mind. Darwin enabled modern secular culture to heave a great collective sigh of relief, by apparently providing a way to eliminate purpose, meaning, and design as fundamental features of the world. Instead they become epiphenomena, generated incidentally by a process that can be entirely explained by the operation of the nonteleological laws of physics on the material of which we and our environments are all composed. There might still be thought to be a religious threat in the existence of the laws of physics themselves, and indeed the existence of anything at all—but it seems to be less alarming to most atheists.

This is a somewhat ridiculous situation. First of all, one should try to resist the intellectual effects of such a fear (if not the fear itself), for it is just as irrational to be influenced in one's beliefs by the hope that God does not exist as by the hope that God does exist. But having said that, I would also like to offer somewhat inconsistently the reassurance that atheists have no more reason to be alarmed by fundamental and irreducible mind-world relations than by fundamental and irreducible laws of physics. It is possible to accept a world view that does not explain everything in terms of quantum field theory without necessarily believing in God. If the natural order can include universal, mathematically beautiful laws of fundamental physics of the kind we have discovered, why can't it include equally fundamental laws and constraints that

9. Colin McGinn makes a related suggestion about the mystery-fearing motives which drive many modern deflationary theories in *Problems in Philosophy* (Blackwell, 1993). But he proposes that the mysteries are a function of our own cognitive limitations, and that itself seems to me, at least with respect to the case of reason, too demystifying.

we don't know anything about, that are consistent with the laws of physics and that render intelligible the development of conscious organisms some of which have the capacity to discover by prolonged collective effort some of the fundamental truths about that very natural order? (I am interpreting the concept of "physics" restrictively enough so that the laws of physics by themselves will not explain the presence of such thinking beings in the space of natural possibilities. Of course, if "physics" just means the most fundamental scientific theory about everything, then it will include any such laws if they exist.)

This need not be a particularly anthropocentric view. We are simply examples of mind, and presumably only one of countless possible, if not actual, rational species on this or other planets. But the existence of mind is certainly a *datum* for the construction of any world picture: At the very least, its *possibility* must be explained. And it seems hardly credible that its appearance should be a natural accident, like the fact that there are mammals.

I admit that this idea—that the capacity of the universe to generate organisms with minds capable of understanding the universe is itself somehow a fundamental feature of the universe—has a quasi-religious "ring" to it, something vaguely Spinozistic. Still, it is this idea, or something like it, which Peirce seems to endorse in the passages I have quoted. And I think one can admit such an enrichment of the fundamental elements of the natural order without going over to anything that should count literally as religious belief. At no point does any of it imply the existence of a divine person, or a world soul.

Actually, I find the religious proposal *less* explanatory than the hypothesis of some systematic aspect of the natural order that would make the appearance of minds in harmony with the universe something to be expected. Here, as elsewhere, the idea of God serves as a placeholder for an explanation where something seems to demand explanation and none is available; that is why so many people welcome Darwinist imperialism. But there is really no reason to assume that the only alternative to an evolutionary explanation of everything is a religious one. However, this may not be comforting enough, because the feeling that I have called the fear of religion may extend far beyond the existence of a personal god, to include any cosmic order of which mind is an irreducible and nonaccidental part. I suspect that there is a deep-seated aversion in the modern "disenchanted" Weltanschauung to any ultimate principles that are not dead—that is, devoid of any reference to the possibility of life or consciousness.

It is unclear what would have to be included in a more mind-friendly cosmology. Even if nature includes laws that explain the *possibility* of intelligent life, those laws won't explain its actuality without the further presence of the right initial conditions. These are specific conditions of the primordial state of our universe that, given its general laws, will lead to the formation of molecules, galaxies, organisms, consciousness, and intelligence. My hypothesis is only that the laws are such as to make not only the first but also the last of these developments intelligible, given the initial conditions that lead to the development of some organisms or other.

II

An evolutionary explanation of human reason is endorsed in Robert Nozick's recent book *The Nature of Rationality*.[10] What he says belongs to the genre of naturalized epistemology, but he uses the evolutionary hypothesis to explain certain limitations on reason, as well as its successes. He proposes a reversal of the Kantian dependence of the facts on reason.

10. Princeton University Press, 1993.

> [I]t is *reason* that is the dependent variable, shaped by the
> facts, and its dependence upon the facts explains the cor-
> relation and correspondence between them. It is just such
> an alternative that our evolutionary hypothesis presents.
> Reason tells us about reality because reality shapes reason,
> selecting for what seems "evident."[11]

Though its full development is extremely interesting, I won't
be concerned with the details of the hypothesis, only with its
status. Here is Nozick's metacomment:

> The evolutionary explanation itself is something we arrive
> at, in part, by the use of reason to support evolutionary
> theory in general and also this particular application of it.
> Hence it does not provide a reason-independent justifica-
> tion of reason, and, although it grounds reason in facts
> independent of reason, this grounding is not accepted by us
> independently of our reason. Hence the account is not part
> of first philosophy; it is part of our current ongoing scien-
> tific view.[12]

Nozick is operating here with the idea that the facts and reality
are what they are independent of what we think, and I shall
follow him in this. He insists that our finding something self-
evident is no guarantee that it is necessarily true, or true at
all—since the disposition to find it self-evident could have
been an evolutionary adaptation to its being only approxi-
mately, and contingently, true.

The proposal is supposed to be an explanation of reason
but not a justification of it. Although it "grounds" reason in
certain evolutionary facts, this is a causal grounding only:
Those facts are not supposed to provide us with *grounds for
accepting* the validity or reliability of reason. So the explanation is not circular. But what is it intended to provide? It seems

11. *The Nature of Rationality,* p. 112.
12. Ibid., p. 112.

to be a proposal of a possible naturalistic explanation of the existence of reason that would, if it were true, make our reliance on reason "objectively" reasonable—that is, a reliable way of getting at the truth (allowing for the equally important function of reason in correcting and improving its own methods).

But is the hypothesis really *compatible* with continued confidence in reason as a source of knowledge about the nonapparent character of the world? In itself, I believe an evolutionary story tells against such confidence. Without something more, the idea that our rational capacity was the product of natural selection would render reasoning far less trustworthy than Nozick suggests, beyond its original "coping" functions. There would be no reason to trust its results in mathematics and science, for example. (And insofar as the evolutionary hypothesis itself depends on reason, it would be self-undermining.)[13]

Unless it is coupled with an *independent* basis for confidence in reason, the evolutionary hypothesis is threatening rather than reassuring. It is consistent with continued confidence only if it amounts to the hypothesis that evolution has led to the existence of creatures, namely us, with a capacity for reasoning in whose validity we can have much *stronger* confidence than would be warranted merely from its having come into existence in that way. I have to be able to believe that the

13. I'm not sure I fully understand Nozick's position. He acknowledges that "Enhancement of inclusive fitness yields selection for approximate truth rather than strict truth" (p. 113). But he then goes on to say that we can self-consciously sharpen our methods once we know this. My problem is, what are we supposed to rely on for this knowledge and these revisions?

The difficulties of evolutionary epistemology are thoroughly explored by Alvin Plantinga in chapter 12 of *Warrant and Proper Function* (Oxford University Press, 1993). He argues that it is irrational to accept evolutionary naturalism, because if it were true, we would have no reason to rely on the methods by which we arrive at it or any other scientific theory.

evolutionary explanation is consistent with the proposition that I follow the rules of logic because they are correct—not *merely* because I am biologically programmed to do so. But to believe that, I have to be justified independently in believing that they *are* correct. And this I cannot be merely on the basis of my contingent psychological disposition, together with the hypothesis that it is the product of natural selection. I can have no justification for trusting a reasoning capacity I have as a consequence of natural selection, unless I am justified in trusting it simply in itself—that is, believing what it *tells* me, in virtue of the *content* of the arguments it delivers.

If reason is in this way self-justifying, then it is open to us also to speculate that natural selection played a role in the evolution and survival of a species that is capable of understanding and engaging in it. But the recognition of logical arguments as independently valid is a *precondition* of the acceptability of an evolutionary story about the source of that recognition. This means that the evolutionary hypothesis is acceptable only if reason does not need its support. At most it may show why the existence of reason need not be biologically mysterious.

The only form that genuine reasoning can take consists in seeing the validity of the arguments, in virtue of what they say. As soon as one tries to step outside of such thoughts, one loses contact with their true content. And one cannot be outside and inside them at the same time: If one *thinks* in logic, one cannot simultaneously regard those thoughts as mere psychological dispositions, however caused or however biologically grounded. If one decides that some of one's psychological dispositions are, as a contingent matter of fact, reliable methods of reaching the truth (as one may with perception, for example), then in doing so one must rely on other thoughts that one actually *thinks*, without regarding them as mere dispositions. One cannot embed all one's reasoning in a psychological theory, including the reasonings that have led to that psychological theory. The epistemological buck must stop somewhere. By this I mean not that there must be some premises that are forever unrevisable but, rather, that in any process of reasoning or argument there must be some thoughts that one simply thinks from the inside—rather than thinking of them as biologically programmed dispositions.

So my conclusion about an evolutionary explanation of rationality is that it is necessarily incomplete. Even if one believes it, one has to believe in the independent validity of the reasoning that is the result.

None of this is to deny that our capacity to reason had survival value (though God knows, plenty of species have survived perfectly well without it). At any rate, it has certainly enabled us to dominate the planet and wipe out most of our competitors and predators, as well as a lot of innocent bystanders. Rationality in our case, at least, has not been extinguished and may have been extended by the mechanism of natural selection. (And it may have been distorted by natural selection: Compare Nozick's hypothesis about why Euclidean geometry seems to us self-evident, even though it is not strictly true of physical space.[14]) I am denying only that what rationality is can be understood through the theory of natural selection. What it is, what it tells us, and what its limits are can be understood only from inside it.

But that leaves the question, how can we integrate such an attitude toward reason with the fact that we are members of a biological species whose evolution has been shaped by the contingencies of natural selection? To this I don't have a proper positive response, only a defensive one: Natural selection has to operate on the biological possibilities that are actualized, and we do not really know how those possibilities and their likelihoods of actualization are constrained by the funda-

14. *The Nature of Rationality*, pp. 109-10.

mental laws of nature. In spite of the evidence that the entire biological creation, including ourselves, is the product of a stupendously long sequence of chance chemical events,[15] the story is radically incomplete in two ways. First, there is so far nothing but speculation about why the space of physico-chemical possibilities contains this path, and how likely it was, given the physical state of the early universe, that some path of this very broad kind would be followed. Since it did happen, it must have been possible, but that may be for reasons we do not yet understand. Perhaps the evolution of the universe and of life operates on a much more constrained set of options than our present knowledge of physics would enable us to imagine. Second, the physical story, without more, cannot explain the mental story, including consciousness and reason.

I suppose it is possible that rationality—the capacity to recognize objectively valid reasons and arguments—is a distinctively accessible member of the set of biological possibilities, one that becomes likely at sufficiently high levels of biological complexity—much more likely than would be predictable on the basis of random mutation and natural selection alone. Like the possibility of molecules or the possibility of consciousness, the possibility of rationality could be a fundamental feature of the natural order.[16] So it is not *inconsistent* to regard ourselves as rational in this sense and also as creatures who have been produced through Darwinian evolution. On the other hand, as I have said, the theory of evolution as usually understood provides absolutely no *support* for this

15. Like most laymen, I have learned whatever I know about current evolutionary theory from popular writings, especially those of Richard Dawkins: *The Selfish Gene* (Oxford University Press, 1976), *The Blind Watchmaker* (W. W. Norton, 1986), and *River out of Eden* (Basic Books, 1995).

16. But as Mark Johnston has said to me, if one asks, "*Why* is the natural order such as to make the appearance of rational beings likely?" it is very difficult to imagine any answer to the question that is not teleological.

conception of ourselves, and to some extent it renders the conception suspect.[17]

An argument to the contrary would require two things. First, it would be necessary to analyze the kind of human rationality that makes possible both the creation and understanding of scientific and mathematical knowledge. What are the component processes of abstraction and inference and grasp of complex logical structures that in combination produce the results of human intelligence, when applied to widely different subject matters? Perhaps a general analysis of the phenomenon into a limited set of functional elements could be carried out, though I suppose it is also possible that there is no such analysis. Second, it would be necessary to consider the relation between this set of capacities and the simpler habits of mind that might plausibly have carried selective advantage in the period when the human brain evolved. It is conceivable, though at first glance not very likely, that the first set of operations might be understood as nothing more than the piling up and recombination and repetition of the members of the second set, applied successively to the results of previous operations using only the same basic mental tools.

But even if such speculations reduce the apparent clash between rationality and natural selection, they cannot underwrite our use of reason. Whatever justification reason provides must come from the reasons it discovers, themselves. They cannot get their authority from natural selection.

So we are left with a profound problem. Can we engage in reasoning in the way we inevitably do without disregarding the radical biological contingency of the human species and

17. Philip Kitcher also rejects an evolutionary defense of reasoning; see *The Advancement of Science* (Oxford University Press, 1993), pp. 300–1. The book is mainly an argument against Kuhn-inspired relativism, notable for its supererogatory patience and for the detailed examination of historical examples of scientific progress.

the human mind? I think there is a conflict here that remains unresolved. The reliance we put on our reason implies a belief that even though the existence of human beings and of ourselves in particular is the result of a long sequence of physical and biological accidents, and even though there might never have come to be any intelligent creatures at all, nevertheless the basic methods of reasoning we employ are not merely human but belong to a more general category of *mind*. Human minds now exemplify it, but those same methods and arguments would have to be among the capacities of any species that had evolved to the level of thinking—even if there were no vertebrates, and a civilization of mollusks or arthropods ruled the earth.

III

What about ethics, and practical reasoning more generally? There a reductively evolutionary explanation of our deepest dispositions, of what we find self-evident or not in need of further justification, is not directly self-defeating. We can think it, relying only on our theoretical reasoning capacities to get "outside" of our ethical and practical judgments. That appears to be true even though we must also remain inside the standpoint of practical reason at least to the extent necessary to make decisions. So here we are faced with two genuine competing hypotheses, the evolutionary and the rationalist. But we are not forced in this case any more than in the other either to accept a debunking evolutionary account or else to deny that our species is the product of natural selection. Practical reason, like theoretical reason, may be among the fundamental biological possibilities on which natural selection operates, and we may be instances of it.

In this case we can do no more than see whether the external view is more convincing than the internal content of practical and moral argument. For example, does it make sense to say that race would be an irrelevant ground for discrimination even if we were intuitively convinced that it was relevant and that it brought the need for further justification to an end? If we say that it would be irrelevant nonetheless, and if we also believe that that answer cannot itself be regarded merely as the manifestation of a disposition whose causes are ultimately biological, then we will be opting for a rationalist conception. We will be relying on our moral reasoning in itself, in virtue of its content and independently of its biological sources.

I think the right way to react to the cruder suggestions of the sociobiological outlook is to consider the alleged biological causes of this or that motivational disposition, and then go on to ask whether, if those are the facts, we are justified in continuing to act on it. There might well be an innate, biologically explicable disposition to racism, for example, yet that does not exempt racism from moral criticism.

But what if the tests of impartiality and mutual justifiability that lead us to count race as objectively irrelevant to how people should be treated could themselves be explained, in their appeal to us, through a further evolutionary story? Would that not then deprive those arguments of their standing as criticisms of racism—unless it could be claimed that they were somehow also objectively correct? Or could we be content just to discover that they weighed more heavily with us than the feelings against which they were directed—regarding this as a brute psychological fact about ourselves which no doubt had its own evolutionary (or perhaps cultural) explanation?

What does it mean to say that my practical reasonings are efforts to get the objectively right answer about what I should do, rather than manifestations of biologically selected dispositions that have no more objective validity than a taste for sugar? The idea of a harmony between thought and reality is no help here, because realism about practical reasons and ethics is not a thesis about the natural order at all, but a purely normative claim. It seems that the response to evolutionary naturalism in this domain must be almost purely negative. All one can say is that justification for actions is to be sought in the content of practical reasoning, and that evolutionary explanation of our dispositions to accept such arguments may undermine our confidence in them but cannot provide a justification for accepting them. So if evolutionary naturalism is the whole story about what we take to be practical reasoning, then there really is no such thing.

Perhaps this will not worry many people; the response may be that we are then left free simply to be ourselves. But it is an attitude toward decision and evaluation that clashes with my (natural) Kantian intuitions. And I suspect that for most people, it is really inconsistent with what they do—even though, as with antirealism in other domains, it is perfectly possible to accompany the continuation of substantively realistic thought and judgment with ritualistic metacomments declaring one's allegiance to subjectivism, relativism, or whatever. Still, the supposition that there are no objective values seems intelligible in a way that the supposition that there are no facts of any kind is not—and it seems to be one possible respect in which one might, however mistakenly, come to regard oneself as a *mere* biological product.

Once innocence has been lost and reflective consciousness has begun, however, there is no way back to a merely biological view of one's own thoughts in general—nor a merely psychological, or sociological, or economic, or political view. All such external forms of understanding are themselves examples of thought, and in the end, any understanding we may achieve of the contingency, subjectivity, and arbitrariness of our desires, impressions, and intuitions (whether or not it is accompanied by acceptance) has to depend on thoughts that are not so qualified—thoughts whose validity is impersonal and whose claim to our assent rests on their content alone.

It is natural to look for a way in which our understanding of the world could close over itself by including us and our methods of thought and understanding within its scope. That is what drives the search for naturalistic accounts of reasoning. But it is also clear that this hope cannot be realized, because the primary position will always be occupied by our *employment* of reason and understanding, and that will be true even when we make reasoning the object of our investigation. So an external understanding of reason as merely another natural phenomenon—a biological product, for example—is impossible. Reason is whatever we find we must *use* to understand anything, including itself. And if we try to understand it merely as a natural (biological or psychological) phenomenon, the result will be an account incompatible with our use of it and with the understanding of it we have in using it. For I cannot *trust* a natural process unless I can see why it is reliable, any more than I can trust a mechanical algorithm unless I can see why it is reliable. And to see that I must rely on reason itself.

Once we enter the world for our temporary stay in it, there is no alternative but to try to decide what to believe and how to live, and the only way to do that is by trying to decide what is the case and what is right. Even if we distance ourselves from some of our thoughts and impulses, and regard them from outside, the process of trying to place ourselves in the world leads eventually to thoughts that we cannot think of as merely "ours." If we think at all, we must think of ourselves, individually and collectively, as submitting to the order of reasons rather than creating it.

INDEX